MULTICULTURAL RELATIONS ON CAMPUS
A Personal Growth Approach

Woodrow M. Parker, Ph.D.
Professor of Education
Department of Counselor Education
University of Florida
Gainesville, Florida

James Archer, Jr., Ph.D.
Director, Counseling Center
Professor of Counselor Education & Psychology
University Counseling Center
University of Florida
Gainesville, Florida

James E. Scott, Ph.D.
Dean of Student Affairs
Student Services
University of Florida
Gainesville, Florida

ACCELERATED DEVELOPMENT
A member of the Taylor & Francis Group
1900 Frost Road, Suite 101
Bristol, PA 19007-1598

MULTICULTURAL RELATIONS ON CAMPUS: A PERSONAL GROWTH APPROACH

Copyright 1992 by Accelerated Development Inc.

10   9   8   7   6   5   4   3

Modifications added after initial printing

Printed in the United States of America

All rights reserved. No part of this book may be reproduced or transmitted in any form or means, electronic or mechanical, including photocopying, recording, or by an informational storage and retrieval system, without permission in writing from Accelerated Development Inc.

Cover Design: Tracey Flanagan

Technical Development: Tanya Benn
Cynthia Long
Marguerite Mader
Sheila Sheward

LCN: 92-52504

ISBN: 1-55959-033-5

Order additional copies from:

ACCELERATED DEVELOPMENT
A member of the Taylor & Francis Group
1900 Frost Road, Suite 101
Bristol, PA 19007-1598
1-800-821-8312

DEDICATIONS

Many individuals contributed to the development of this book. Therefore, thanks are extended to the Counseling Center staff members and students at Florida State University and the University of Florida for gathering and providing information essential for writing several chapters in this book.

I also would like to express appreciation to my wife, Liz, my sons, Eldridge and Torrey, and my daughters, Toyake and Farha, for their encouragement and support throughout this project.

W.M. Parker

This book is dedicated to Tony Rodriquez, one of my best friends at Horace Mann Junior High School in Denver, Colorado. Tony helped me learn to challenge stereotypes and to make decisions about people based on my own judgements.

J. Archer

This book is dedicated to my three children, Lori, James II, and Jason.

J.E. Scott

PREFACE

The program for multicultural awareness presented in this book, for the most part, will be fun. Learning more about yourself and about how relationships and communication between different groups of people can be improved is exciting. Yes, you may experience anger and sadness at times, but this will be part of a process that leads to growth.

We don't really intend this book to be political. We realize, of course, that political forces cannot be ignored and that institutional racism is a significant problem in our colleges and universities. We have chosen to focus this program on the individual student and his or her own multicultural attitudes. We are confident that most students want to learn more about themselves and their attitudes toward diverse groups. We believe that as individual students become more sensitive to diversity and cultural differences, they will be motivated to help fight racism and prejudice on college campuses.

The program outlined in this book requires the organizers, teachers, and trainers of the course or workshop to gather a group of diverse participants. A great deal of the learning involves students hearing from and learning about people who are different from themselves. One of the most basic ways to break stereotypes is to get to know people from the group being stereotyped.

We wish you the best as you embark on your journey to become a more culturally effective person. We admire your willingness to participate and we commend you for your openness to new experiences and ideas. Your participation will help you become a more competent and effective person and you will be better able to face the challenges of our increasingly diverse society in the 21st century.

TABLE OF CONTENTS

3 STEREOTYPING 51

4 EMPATHY AND AWARENESS OF CAMPUS MINORITIES 65

5 BECOMING A CULTURALLY EFFECTIVE PERSON: DEVELOPING SENSITIVITY 87

LIST OF ACTIVITIES

LIST OF FIGURES

Chapter 1

INTRODUCTION

A young man in tears comes in to a Dean's office reporting that all of his belongings have been pushed out into the hall and that a sign has been placed on the door to his dorm room warning, "Fags Keep Out."

A Black student tells a friend that one of his professors never calls on him in class. "Does the professor think I'm stupid?" he asks.

A Chinese American student overhears some friends talking about her. "Those Orientals are all such grinds, they really bring up the curve."

A Black student reports nonchalantly to a discussion group that someone scribbled "nigger" on his door last week. "It's not the first time," he says.

A Jewish student, who previously thought JAP (Jewish American Princess) jokes were funny, sees a T-shirt that reads, "Slap a JAP," and begins to worry about anti-Semitic violence.

Are these isolated incidents or is racism and cultural insensitivity still a major problem on our college and university campuses? Steele (1989), in an article on campus racism, reviewed the two major incidents a few years ago at the University of Massachusetts and at Dartmouth. Examples were cited at Yale, the University of Wisconsin, UC Berkeley,

UCLA, Stanford, and "countless other" incidents that have propelled Black students to protest.

What do these major racial incidents at some of our finest universities mean? Has affirmative action created a backlash for minorities? Has the conservative swing in the country during the 1980s led to less concern about fairness and equality and a regression to earlier days of intolerance and prejudice? Jon Wiener (1989), writing in *The Nation*, concluded that the "legitimization" of racism during the Reagan years is an important factor.

Although some campuses have not had overt racial or cultural conflicts, what seems clear is that issues of racism, prejudice, and stereotyping are still very much a part of the American higher education scene. A Stanford University Report, *Building a Multiracial Multicultural University Community*, was written by a study committee at Stanford, partly out of concern about increasing acts of racism and intolerance. Authors of the report help clarify the development of multicultural attitudes on campuses with one of their conclusions: "Today, we have achieved unprecedented racial and ethnic diversity, especially in the undergraduate student body . . . Now we must make the transition from numerical diversity to interactive pluralism."

Charles Taylor (1986), in an article comparing Black student perceptions as reported by Frederick Harper in 1969 with those of current (1986) Black students, suggested rather limited progress for Black students.

> Being Black is to go into class disadvantaged and find that I have a teacher who believes it is impossible for a Black student to make an A or B grade. (Harper, 1969, in Taylor, 1986)

> Being Black is to go to class thinking I am well prepared, but for the life of me I cannot figure out why the teacher gave me a C when I know I deserved a B. The White students who asked me for help and did less work got an A, but I still do not understand why I got a C. (Taylor, 1986, p. 197)

Hughes (1987) reported a decrease in Black enrollment in higher education from 1976 to 1983. She concluded after studying a group of Black college students that

> Both Black men and Black women are aware that most predominantly White universities are not necessarily healthy environments for their development. Nurturance, confidence building, and positive identity formations are stifled on these campuses. An environment filled with prejudices and stereotypes provokes tentativeness, suspicion, restriction, and harsh self-examination. (Hughes, 1987, p. 543)

The situation for other minorities is also not much improved. A decrease may have occurred in overt hostility (although many instances continue to occur), but the previously hoped-for communication and understanding between different racial and ethnic groups have not materialized. Hispanic, Native American, and to some extent Jewish and Asian students continue to be isolated. Majority-culture students often have limited knowledge and understanding of other cultures and of the more subtle aspects of racism and cultural practices of others.

Although many examples exist, one that has received attention recently is the stereotyping of Jewish students as a result of the widespread use of the term JAP (Jewish American Princess). In some of the northeastern schools where Jewish populations are significant, overt antagonisms have been expressed. For example, T-shirts that have anti-JAP and in some cases violent phrases about this stereotype are not unusual. Other groups, such as Asians, Hispanics, Native Americans, and African-Americans are also frequent recipients of prejudice and stereotyping.

Gay and Lesbian students are also frequent recipients of hostility. Although some campuses have functioning Gay and Lesbian organizations, great fear exists among these students regarding the consequences of "coming out." The onset of AIDS has probably had a negative impact on attitudes toward Gay males.

Cross-racial and cross-cultural understanding among students on college campuses is typically viewed as an important educational goal. Most colleges and universities have a statement in their catalogues about the importance of learning from others and from other cultures, yet relationships among various campus racial and cultural groups and cultural understanding of different groups often need improvement. Fraternities and sororities are divided into Black, White, and Jewish, and an overtly Gay or Lesbian student cannot usually be accepted as a member of any Greek organization.

Certainly one cannot single out colleges and universities as necessarily responsible for intolerance and lack of cross-cultural understanding. They have, however, largely failed in their mission to teach their students a better and more pluralistic way of understanding different races, cultures, and other minorities. The problem is not a simple one and, as Saenger (1953) cautioned many years ago, there is no one single way to reduce prejudice and discrimination.

Most college students in the 1990s will enter a work force in transition upon their graduation. Only 15% of the new entrants to the labor market for the duration of this century will be white males. The others will be racial and ethnic minorities, women, and new immigrants. This shift in the demographic constitution of the work force will impact the organization cultures of the American work place, and will be an important factor in the career success of college graduates.

In addition to attaining knowledge and skills related to specific occupations, students have a vested interest in increasing their sensitivity to, and conforming with, persons from varied backgrounds. Students who become culturally effective are likely to have greater mastery of their work environment and more influence over work associates than individuals who are culturally encapsulated. These abilities can be critical success factors in a career, and may separate tomorrow's leaders from their followers.

Over the past few years a number of attempts have been made to reduce interracial and intercultural tension and anxiety, and to improve contact and communication among various racial and cultural groups. One approach has been based on the premise that knowledge about other groups' cultural and historical backgrounds would improve communication and relations. Very little evidence can be found that this knowledge improves attitudes and communication. In fact, Lloyd (1987) contended that to be uninformed is better than to be informed. He suggested that when people begin to make certain assumptions from what they know of groups, they often stereotype and lose the individuality of the persons with whom they are interacting. In this case, a little knowledge may be a dangerous thing.

GENERAL APPROACH

This book is designed to improve racial and cultural sensitivity on predominantly White campuses, through a structured learning approach. Although some progress has been made since the 1960s, the authors feel strongly that serious problems still exist and that these problems of insensitivity, misconception, misunderstanding, and sometimes hate must be addressed. Our primary goal is to develop culturally sensitive persons (CSP's). Individuals (faculty, students, and staff) who are culturally sensitive themselves can be a significant positive force on their campuses. Our approach is a very personal one, with the individual as the target of training and change. We believe strongly in the individual's role as an agent for change within the institution.

Although we emphasize individual change, we realize that very serious systemic and institutional problems do exist. One cannot begin to develop culturally sensitive people without running head-on into institutional racism and other problems. In a sense, the question is "Where to start?" Since individuals can control and change an institution, one appropriate place is with these individuals.

As was mentioned previously, many multicultural training models have taken a "learn about minorities" approach. We take a somewhat different one, although we do believe in the value of increased knowledge about minorities. We favor a relatively gentle yet confrontive approach that emphasizes personal awareness, self-knowledge, and honest communication among majority and minority students. We are attempting to improve personal attitudes and behaviors with the belief that this will greatly aid the cause of better multicultural relationships on campuses. Although some of the attitudes and behaviors of intolerant students are strongly offensive and damaging, high-pressure tactics and guilt slinging, in our judgment, do not serve the cause of personal attitude change. We do not mean to ignore the power and institutional realities, and we also favor more political, high visibility tactics that might be appropriate for systemic and institutional change.

DEFINITIONS

Before proceeding further, the issue of how one defines "minority" needs to be confronted. We have racial, ethnic, sexual orientation, and many other minority groups on our campuses. Also the question of gender must be considered. Women are often considered a minority because of the general powerlessness that they have experienced in the past. Although we do not have material and activities to highlight all the different minorities in this book, we hope that the process of examining attitudes toward minorities will generalize. In our definitions we have included Gay/Lesbian students as a cultural minority. Although they are often not a visible minority, their oppression by society has in some ways forced the creation of a kind of separate culture. We have not conceptualized this book and program as being specifically useful in dealing with sex role issues, nor do we have material geared toward physically disabled student minorities.

A number of other definitions also will be utilized:

> **Racial Minority:** Refers to groups who are identified by distinctive physical characteristics perceived differently from those of other members of a society. Skin color, hair type, body structure, and/or shape of head, nose, or eyes are often singled out as different. Racial refers to biological traits or qualities.

> **Ethnic Minority:** A group who shares common characteristics, customs, and traditions that are

different from those of the majority group. In addition, they have often been psychologically and geographically separated from the majority culture, which often causes them to develop their own life-style. A group obtains ethnic status through social relations and interactions. Some representatives of American ethnic minorities are Jewish, Hispanic, Black, Asian, and Native American.

Minority: A group whose population is composed of less than one-half the size of the total population.

Culturally Different Group: Any group whose life-style, values, customs, traditions, language, and/or cultural practices are different from your own. Gay and Lesbian students are included in this category.

Cross-cultural Communication: Any interaction involving two or more speakers who are different from one another based on ethnicity, race, religion, or sexual orientation.

Ethnocentrism: A basic human survival response. It is the belief that one's group (family, country, culture, belief system) is right and must be defended.

Multicultural Setting: Any place, agency, or institution where culturally different group members make up a portion of the population.

Culturally Effective Persons (CEP's): Individuals who are sensitive to the needs, issues, and concerns of culturally diverse group members. CEP's develop sensitivity through extensive life experiences with ethnic minorities or through special training.

Prejudice: An emotional response, usually based on fear, mistrust, and/or ignorance, which is directed at a racial, religious, national, or other cultural group.

Stereotype: An overgeneralization applied to an individual without regard to his or her own uniqueness; e.g., "Men are unemotional, women are weak, Asians are quiet." Stereotypes are difficult to deal with because they sometimes contain kernels of truth. They are often conceptualizations that people use to avoid dealing with one another as individuals.

Racism: The institutionalized practice of excluding groups of people from power solely on the basis of race. Such exclusion takes the form of discrimination, prejudice, segregation, and domination.

"Red-neck Racism": Refers to the practices of those persons who believe that members of a specific cultural group are inferior and not worthy of decent treatment. ("Send them back where they came from.")

Cultural Encapsulation: A process whereby cultural variations in people are disregarded.

Adapted from *Multicultural Education, A Cross Cultural Training Approach*, 1979, Margaret D. Pusch, Editor.

TRAINING MODEL

This book is designed as a workbook/text for courses, extended programs, or workshops on cultural sensitivity. It is designed primarily for use by college students, although it can also be used in programs that include faculty and administrators. Since one of our basic assumptions is that participants will learn from each other, many of the activities and exercises involve interaction among students of different cultural and racial groups. Although students and other members of the academic community can profit from reading and completing some of the activities by themselves, participation in a group approach with different cultural and minority students is preferred.

The model moves from individual awareness to action planning. The specific steps include the following:

1. **Personal Awareness.** The focus here is on exploring and understanding one's own cultural identity and attitudes. Some specific models of minority identity and White racial consciousness are explored and participants examine their own family cultural background.

2. **Stereotyping.** In this step, the process of stereotyping is examined. Examples of labeling, and automatic stereotyping are given, and specific campus stereotypes are identified.

3. **Empathy or Awareness of Campus Minorities.** The role and status of specific campus minorities is examined. Majority students hear directly from minority students about their experiences and perceptions on the campus. Role-plays and other techniques are used to increase empathy.

4. **Developing Sensitivity.** A further examination of campus situations is used here to move students from empathy to increased sensitivity in attitudes and behaviors. Some examination of the campus environment is included here.

5. **Cross-cultural Communication.** Individual communication barriers are addressed here, with a focus on how to overcome those barriers. The issue of minority identity versus contacts with the majority community is addressed here.

6. **Multicultural Action Planning.** In this stage, students develop action plans for the future to improve their own cultural sensitivity and behavior. Campus-wide projects are also discussed and developed.

This book includes a chapter on each of these steps.

GENERAL GOALS

Changing attitudes and behavior that are a result of life-long learning and socialization is not any easy task. Certainly, the possibilities for change in a weekend workshop or weekly course are limited. Nonetheless, the authors are convinced that positive change can occur if students and other members of the academic community will take the time to examine their own attitudes and feelings, and talk with each other about these important issues that are often not addressed until some kind of crisis occurs. We urge you to take this personal growth opportunity. You will be better for it, and you will be able to contribute to a more productive and ethical campus community. Following are some of the specific goals that you can achieve with this program:

1. Increase your understanding of the problems and perceptions of the minority students on your campus.

2. Increase your self-awareness and be able to identify the attitudes that you have developed toward minority and majority groups.

3. Increase your empathy and understanding of minority group culture and behavior.

4. Increase your sensitivity and positive behavior toward racial, ethnic and other minority groups.

5. Increase your knowledge about different minority group cultures, activities, and contributions, and motivate yourself to learn more.

6. Improve the campus climate for minority group students and enrich the environment for everyone by increasing communication and interaction among various campus groups.

USING THIS PROGRAM
(Information for Organizers and Facilitators)

We see this program as usable on any college or university campus. It is relatively nonthreatening, generally fun, and fairly easy to administer. We feel that a course, a weekend retreat with follow-up meetings, or an extended workshop are probably the most effective formats. Getting away from the campus and using a retreat center can add an atmosphere and opportunity for informal interaction that is very helpful. The program does include information and activities that can be done individually; but, as previously mentioned, the best results come from working in racially and culturally mixed groups.

Students, faculty, and staff can participate. However, the program is designed primarily for students. If others participate in a workshop or course, care must be taken that faculty and staff participants do not overshadow the student participants. When the idea of a course or workshop is introduced to the campus, significant participation by all minority groups is essential. A planning group or steering committee representing all the campus minority and majority groups is a good place to start. All groups must have some ownership of the activity for it to draw students.

When the program is to be used in a course or workshop, the over-all workshop leader should be an experienced teacher and facilitator, and small group leaders with some experience are helpful. Specially trained students, or perhaps graduate students in counseling, psychology, or social work, are often available. The planning or steering committee is a good source for group leaders. The president or administration of the institution must give support and financial backing. Often student groups have more success in approaching these officials for financial support.

Timing of a weekend retreat or extended workshop sessions is quite important. Unless a weekend retreat is held early in the term, when a number of competing events is not occurring, obtaining student participants will be difficult. Extended workshop sessions need to be held at times when students can attend. A course format for extended sessions is useful as a way of building in a regular commitment for attendance and participation. Participation by majority groups like fraternities and sororities should be encouraged. Personal invitations are helpful. The broader the cross-section of students, the more learning will occur. Organizers should avoid "preaching to the choir." That is, attempts must be made to include students who would not normally volunteer for this kind of activity.

ACTIVITY 1-1
JOURNAL WRITING ACTIVITY

We encourage you to take some time after reading each chapter and participating in the activities to think about your own feelings and reactions. One good way to do this is to keep a journal. You don't have to be an English major or an aspiring writer to do this. The quality and form of the writing are not really important. What is important is your taking the time to try to put down on paper some of your reactions.

Objectives

1. To encourage reflection and awareness.

2. To increase the quality of learning and group discussion.

Directions to Group Leaders

If possible, provide time for journal entry during various phases of the training program. If this is offered as a course or extended workshop, group leaders or trainers may want to collect journals periodically. Students should be informed beforehand if this system will be used.

Directions to Participants

If you have never tried a journal or a diary before, you will be amazed at how helpful it can be. In a way, you are forcing yourself to clarify ideas and feelings. When you get them on paper, seeing what you have written often helps you understand, accept, and appreciate issues that you are confronting. Some recent psychological studies have even shown that journal writing can help your mental health!

So, give it a try! Obtain a small notebook and start a journal. Remember that you, and possibly your trainer, will be the only one who sees your journal. Be honest, don't worry about the format or your writing style. Try to confront, explain, and understand your feelings and reactions.

If you need help in structuring your journal, consider the following format:

ISSUE I AM CONFRONTING

REACTION TO CHAPTER/IDEA
—Thoughts
—Feelings
—Explanations
—Ideas
—Hypotheses
—Possible Action/Behavior Change

REFERENCES

Hughes, M.S. (1987). Black students' participation in higher education. *Journal of College Student Personnel, 28,* 532-545

Lloyd, A. (1987). Multicultural counseling: Does it belong in a counselor education program? *Counselor Education and Supervision, 26,* 164-167.

Pusch, M.D. (1979). A cross-cultural training approach. *Multicultural Education, Vol. 8,* p. 276.

Saenger, G. (1953). *The social psychology of prejudice.* New York: Harper and Brothers.

Steele, S. (1989, February). The recoloring of campus life, *Harpers,* 47-55.

Taylor, C. (1986). Black students on predominantly White college campuses in the 1980's. *Journal of College Student Personnel, 27,* 146-202.

Wiener, J. (1989, February 27). Racial hatred on campus. *The National,* 260-263.

Chapter **2**

PERSONAL AWARENESS: IDENTITY DEVELOPMENT AND MULTICULTURAL RELATIONS

The purpose of this chapter is to increase personal awareness of your own racial and cultural background and to provide you with some understanding of the importance of race and ethnic background in identity formation. These goals will be achieved through a discussion of a racial and ethnic identification (including two models of ethnic identity development). In addition, a model of gay or lesbian identity development will be identified and discussed. The chapter will conclude with a series of activities designed to facilitate your self-awareness and exploration of your ideas and feelings concerning these issues.

RACIAL AND ETHNIC IDENTIFICATION: A VEHICLE FOR SELF-UNDERSTANDING

What is the first thing you think when you see a bi-racial couple holding hands? Or what is your reaction to men who are clearly engaged in a gay relationship? What causes your reactions? Do you think others may feel differently? One way to understand your reaction is to explore your racial or cultural background and/or your attitude toward gays and lesbians. Some social scientists believe our ethnic and racial identity and our attitudes toward sexual orientation are powerful because they represent many hidden forces we often cannot identify, but know exist (Smith, 1985). These forces are similar to what Sue (1978) referred to as a world view. "World view constitutes our psychological orientation in life and can determine how we think, behave, make decisions, and define events" (p. 458). The way we perceive our relationship to nature, institutions, and other people and things is all influenced by our world view. We are often unaware of the impact of these forces on our day-to-day feelings and responses to people we encounter on campus.

How do we acquire our racial and ethnic identity? Helms (1984) contended that all people, regardless of race or ethnic origin, go through a stage-wise process of developing racial and ethnic consciousness. This process is a part of personal growth and comes about as a result of our effort to understand and integrate our life experiences. An examination of your own racial or ethnic development can help you better understand the nature of your attitudes and feelings toward people unlike yourself.

Three models of identity development will be examined here. The first is the Minority Identity Development Model advanced by Atkinson, Morten, and Sue (1979); the second is described as the White Racial Consciousness Model (Helms, 1984); and the third model is for Gay and Lesbian Identity Development advanced by Cass (1979). These models are described in some detail so that you (minority, majority, and gay or lesbian participants) can evaluate your own developmental progress.

MINORITY IDENTITY DEVELOPMENT MODEL

The Minority Identity Developmental Model (MID) has five stages: (1) conformity, (2) dissonance, (3) resistance and immersion, (4) introspection, and (5) synergetic articulation and awareness (Atkinson et al., 1979). Each stage is associated with an attitude involving the self, others, and the dominant group. Minority individuals evolve through these stages as they encounter experiences in which their race or ethnic affiliation is a factor. Since people's life experiences and reactions differ, this model should be viewed as a vehicle and a structure for exploring racial and ethnic identity, rather than as a rigid predictor of identity development.

Stage One: Conformity

In this stage, ethnic minorities identify strongly with the White dominant society, permitting the White society to define their worth and value, and to determine their life directions. Such persons idealize Whites and hold negative feelings toward their own ethnic group. Individuals in this stage often accept negative stereotypes about themselves and their group. In addition, they know very little and are not interested in learning about their own ethnic heritage or history. Such persons usually associate with White people and have very little to do with members of their own ethnic group.

Stage Two: Dissonance

Many minority persons have experiences, or gain insights, that cause them to question their conforming attitudes, and cause confusion and conflict. They question values of the dominant culture they have previously held in high esteem. They become more aware of racism, oppression, and stereotyping. Some individuals may even become curious about the history of their own cultural group. Feelings of anger, guilt, and loss surface. In this stage, ethnic minority individuals may attempt to develop friendly relations with members of their own ethnic group with whom they have previously not been able to identify.

Sometimes, certain life events influence the racial and cultural identity attitudes of individuals causing a shift in their identity attitudes. For example, Bob, a Cuban student, became more closely identified with his cultural group when other students in his dormitory discovered his ethnic origin. First, a few of his friends began to call him Roberto, his given name, and this made him feel uncomfortable. His cultural identity status was further emphasized when his big family— mother, father, aunts, uncles, grandparents, nieces, and nephews—came to visit him on campus. This visit was characterized by hugs, kisses, fun, laughter, and, in general, a great celebration in a characteristic Cuban fashion. Many of the hall residents were surprised to learn that he was Cuban, that his parents spoke Spanish, and that they engaged in such physical demonstrations of affection. Following this incident, some of the students began to react to Bob differently and to make wisecracks about his family. These attitudes and behaviors caused Bob to take a closer look at himself and to seek out his own ethnic group as a major source of support.

Stage Three: Resistance and Immersion

This stage is characterized by a complete rejection of the dominant culture and a total acceptance of one's own cultural group. This is considered a stage of extremes, during which individuals become immersed in their own cultural history, values, and life-style. Such persons are highly motivated to combat oppression, racism, and prejudice, and may evidence activist behavior and an increased distrust of the dominant culture.

People in this stage often take on a new image that exemplifies their culture. They may change their names, eat only food characteristic to their culture, wear clothes typical of the ethnic group, and participate in causes of special interest to their ethnic group. Overall, these individuals attempt to completely separate themselves from the dominant group, believing that majority people are responsible for their negative life circumstances.

Stage Four: Introspection

In this stage, minority individuals take a hard look at their total rejection of the dominant culture and total acceptance of their own group. These individuals often experience conflict and confusion regarding loyalty to their cultural groups and their personal preferences and autonomy. Internal conflict is most profound in this stage, as individuals struggle to find a balance between what they want for themselves, based on personal desires, needs, and aspirations versus what their own ethnic group expects of them.

The introspection stage involves ethnic minority persons taking a deep look inside themselves and answering some fundamental questions. One of the authors recalls going through this stage and exploring some of the following questions:

1. Was it possible to have an appreciation of both his Black racial group and people of the White majority group?

2. Were there qualities of both groups he would like to incorporate for himself?

3. Were there qualities or life-styles in the Black culture he found undesirable and would like to change?

4. Was it logical to dislike or hate people with whom he was unfamiliar and whom he had never encountered?

5. Was there truth to the saying that "Hate destroys the hater"?

6. Were there negative psychological consequences in harboring feelings of hate?

These questions have no simple answers. The struggle for self-awareness is on-going and is healthy as long as the individual remains open, flexible, and willing to explore these issues and feelings with selected individuals.

Stage Five: Synergetic Articulation and Awareness

This stage offers optimal possibilities for positive multicultural and multiracial communication. Minorities in this stage have resolved many of the previously experienced conflicts, resulting in fulfillment of their cultural identity.

Persons in this stage have acquired knowledge and an appreciation of their own cultural group, which enable them to value and respect the culture and values of other people. Stage Five individuals are secure in their cultural identity, whether it be Black, Hispanic, Native American, or Asian American. Additionally, they recognize that racism, cultural insensitivity, and sexism still exist, and they are willing to deal with it wherever and whenever it occurs in their lives.

This stage is often best exemplified by minorities who are able to function in both minority and majority settings. These individuals have come to terms with, and have gained a greater appreciation of, their own ethnic group. They have often achieved this knowledge through difficult introspection and from positive role models in their cultural groups.

WHITE RACIAL CONSCIOUSNESS MODEL

The second model of identity development is the White Racial Consciousness Model (WRCM) developed by Helms (1984). This model is based on attitudes, feelings, beliefs, and behaviors which White majority individuals hold as a result of their perceptions or actual experiences with Black people living in the American society. The authors believe that the model can be adapted to majority attitudes and behaviors toward minorities other than Blacks. The following description of Helms' (1984) five stages will allow you (White majority individuals) to better understand your racial attitudes and suggest a path for self-actualization as culturally effective persons.

Stage One: Contact

To a large extent, many White people avoid contact with ethnic minority individuals. The individuals have the freedom to either confront their racial and ethnic attitudes or to avoid them altogether.

In the contact stage, White persons become aware that Blacks and other ethnic minorities exist. They approach minority persons with interest and with curiosity. Naivete characterizes interaction with, and knowledge about, ethnic minorities. A tendency exists to ignore racial and cultural differences, or to regard differences as being unimportant.

In the contact stage, White individuals are unaware of themselves as racial beings because being White is so much the norm that it is taken for granted. Those in this stage who choose to interact across racial and cultural lines become aware of societal pressure against doing so.

Individuals may choose to deal with their discomfort by not associating with ethnic minorities (withdrawal) or by continuing to do so (approach). Those who withdraw remain stagnant and may anticipate further interracial difficulties. Those who choose the approach resolution become victims of the social and political ramifications of cross-racial relationships. This awareness often places White people "between a rock and a hard place." They are often confused by reactions from ethnic minorities (minorities who perceive curiosity and interest as paternalistic attitudes) while they are being rejected by their own White group. This condition often moves people into the disintegration stage.

Stage Two: Disintegration

In the disintegration stage, Whites are forced to acknowledge that they are White. According to Katz and Ivey (1977), awareness of racism and prejudice leaves Whites with feelings of guilt and depression. A White student in one of the authors' classes related that his uncle told him to tell any minority job applicant that there were no jobs available, even when there were. This student knew that by lying to all minority applicants he was practicing racism. If he had violated the family's racist norms and hired minority applicants, he might have been seen as disloyal to his family as well as to his racial group. In other words, the individual was caught between internal standards of human decency and external cultural expectations.

According to Helms (1984), the person in the disintegration stage may respond to the dilemma in three different ways: (a) overidentification with ethnic minorities, (b) paternalistic attitudes toward ethnic minorities, or (c) retreat back into the White culture. Those who overidentify experience extreme difficulty because they are often rejected by the minority group, and finally realize that they cannot truly become a member of that group. Paternalism also does not work because White people attempting to take care of minority people often do not receive the appreciation they expect for their efforts. As White individuals attempt to cope with this interpersonal rejection, they may enter the reintegration stage.

Stage Three: Reintegration

Individuals in this stage may become very hostile toward ethnic minorities and become more positively biased toward their own group. This group is considered racially and culturally prejudiced. They are either covertly or overtly anti-ethnic. Many Stage Three individuals perceive ethnic minority traits as negative. They are both angry and afraid.

Individuals who withdraw at this point might remain stuck until some societal pressure forces them to interact with ethnic minorities. Conversely, individuals who accept their Whiteness and become more personally aware of their feelings and attitudes about being White begin to understand the political ramifications of being a White person in a predominantly White society. Their anger, fear, and guilt dissipate and they may enter the pseudo-independent stage.

Stage Four: Pseudo-Independence

This stage is characterized by an intellectual acceptance of ethnic minority persons. Often an increasing interest in and a respect for racial and cultural-group similarities and differences prevail. A pronounced feature of this stage is that, while cross-cultural communication occurs, it involves those minorities who are most similar to Whites. For example, ethnic minorities with comparable values, educational and economic levels, and with sometimes similar physical features to White people, might be invited to socialize with White people. One such minority person—a young, light-skinned, articulate, college professor—told one of the authors that so many White people were inviting him to dinner that he hardly had time to do much of anything else. He was scheduled to have dinners in the homes of White people for more than three months in advance.

While the pseudo-independent stage is characterized by cross-racial involvement on an intellectual level, emotionally significant experiences with ethnic minorities can facilitate attitude change and movement to an advanced stage.

Stage Five: Autonomy

In the autonomy stage, White individuals have greater acceptance of racial differences and similarities. Helms (1984) characterized this stage best, stating, "Differences are not perceived as deficits and similarities are not perceived as enhancers" (p. 156). Members of either racial group are accepted as individuals, but autonomous people actively seek opportunities to involve themselves in cross-cultural interaction because they value cultural diversity and are secure in their own ethnic identity.

GAY AND LESBIAN
IDENTITY DEVELOPMENT

Similar to the MID (Minority Identity Development Model) and the WRCM (White Racial Consciousness Model), a stage identity development model exists for Gay and Lesbian students. According to Fassinger (1991) the development of gay and lesbian identity and the process of "coming out" is lengthy, difficult, and complicated by gender, race, culture, social class, religion, and geographic location. Cass (1979) presented a six stage model.

Stage One: Identity Confusion

Individuals in this stage begin to pay attention to information on sexual orientation and being gay or lesbian, and to realize that some of their thoughts, behavior, or feelings may be similar to those of gay and lesbian people. Feelings about this realization vary, but eventually awareness grows to the point where it can't be ignored. A sense of incongruence (conflict between their perception of themselves as heterosexual and realization of gay or lesbian thoughts and feelings) develops.

People generally react in one of three ways. First, they may seek more information about being gay or lesbian and same sex attraction through books, counseling, or other sources. This new information typically increases the incongruence. Second, they may deny their earlier awareness and attempt to insulate themselves from any information about sexual orientation, and stop any behavior or feelings toward members of the same sex. Third, they may adopt a very anti-gay/lesbian stand, an asexual approach, or increase their heterosexual activity. They may have same sexual contacts, but they tend to define them as experimenting.

Individuals in this stage rarely disclose their concerns to others because their issues are still unclear and confusing. If they successfully reject or deny same sex behaviors and feeling, then, identity foreclosure occurs. This means that they no longer consciously consider a gay or lesbian identity.

Stage Two: Identity Comparison

In this stage the person begins to accept the possibility of having a predominately gay or lesbian orientation, and moves from confusion and incongruence toward addressing the social alienation resulting from a commitment to being gay or lesbian. This alienation and loss of familiar life structures may lead to attempts at therapy to deal with this alienation.

Individuals continue to present a public image of heterosexuality and may try to cope with alienation by trying to be asexual or heterosexual and rejecting same sex feelings and behavior. When this approach is successful the personal gay or lesbian identity is foreclosed and they are typically left with considerable self-hate.

Stage Three: Identity Tolerance

In this stage the person begins to admit to him or herself that he or she is probably gay or lesbian. This helps the person decrease identity confusion and allows him or her to pursue more of his or her own emotional, social, and sexual needs. On the other hand, it accentuates the difference between his or her internal sense of self and the public persona. In this stage the person seeks out contacts and friends in the gay or lesbian community and has a chance to see positive role models. If the contacts are positive, he or she will probably become more accepting of a gay or lesbian sexual identity and move toward a stronger self-statement that, "I am gay or lesbian."

Stage Four: Identity Acceptance

In this stage the individual increases contact with other gay and lesbian people and accepts a gay or lesbian identity. Issues of "who am I?" and "where do I belong?" are more clearly defined. Incongruity and alienation, however, often continue because of the lack of acceptance by the heterosexual community. The individual may be required to develop certain strategies, i.e., passing, limited contact, and limited disclosure of his or her sexual orientation. The person may be able to fit in with both the gay or lesbian and straight world. For some individuals this strategy works and they successfully live their lives at this stage. For others, the notion of only partial disclosure and the continued hiding moves them into Stage Five.

Stage Five: Identity Pride

Anger at the nonacceptance of the heterosexual world and pride in being gay or lesbian propel the person in this stage to become active in gay and lesbian organizations and often to become an activist working toward fighting discrimination. People at this stage often reject previous strategies used to hide their sexual orientation and often reject heterosexual values and institutions. Personal reactions by heterosexual friends and others in this stage can be both positive and negative. If reactions are generally negative, then the person tends to stay in this stage; however, if they are positive, the person moves into the next and final stage.

Stage Six: Identity Synthesis

In this stage, the "us and them" mentality gives way to a more differentiated view. Feelings of pride continue, but the person comes to recognize that the dichotomy between the gay and straight world is not as clear-cut as he or she previously perceived. Personal and public views of self are synthesized and a person's sexual identity becomes less important as sexual identity is integrated into all other aspects of self.

SUMMARY

In summary, these models of ethnic/racial and gay identity development represent one vehicle through which you, as a minority, majority, or gay/lesbian student, can begin to understand yourself and your relationship to people with different backgrounds from your own. College students from minority, majority, and gay/lesbian backgrounds can become more aware of their similarities and differences. You also can expect to develop a better appreciation of your own and other cultural groups.

Summaries of the three models (Minority Identity Development, White Racial Consciousness and Gay/Lesbian Identity Development) are included in Figure 1, Figure 2, and Figure 3. You will need to understand the models to participate in the first three learning activities. Please review the *Minority Identity Development Model* (MID) (Figure 1), the *White Racial Consciousness Model* (WRCM) (Figure 2), and the *Gay Identity Development Model* (GIDM) (Figure 3) that follow before you move to the learning activity section of this chapter.

Figure 1
MINORITY IDENTITY DEVELOPMENT MODEL
(Adapted from Atkinson, Morten, and Sue, 1979)

STAGE ONE
CONFORMITY STAGE

1. Identifies more strongly with dominant culture values.

2. Lacks awareness of an ethnic perspective.

3. Exhibits negative attitudes toward self and others as part of an ethnic group.

4. Accepts and believes stereotypes prevalent in society about self and group.

STAGE TWO
DISSONANCE STAGE

1. Experiences confusion and conflict about the values and beliefs developed in Stage One.

2. Actively questions dominant culture values.

3. Becomes aware of issues involving racism, sexism, oppression, etc.

4. Identifies with the history of the personal cultural group.

5. Has feelings of anger and loss.

6. Seeks role model from the cultural group to which one belongs.

Figure 1 (Continued)

STAGE THREE
RESISTANCE AND IMMERSION STAGE

1. Actively and forcefully rejects and distrusts the dominant culture.

2. Demonstrates greater identification with own culture group.

3. Immerses into ethnic history, traditions, foods, language, etc.

4. Begins to exhibit activist behavior with motivation toward combating oppression, racism, and sexism.

5. Might separate from the dominant culture.

STAGE FOUR
INTROSPECTION STAGE

1. Questions rigid rejection of dominant culture values.

2. Experiences conflict and confusion regarding loyalty to one's own cultural group and personal autonomy.

3. Struggles for self-awareness continuously.

STAGE FIVE
SYNERGETIC ARTICULATION AND
AWARENESS STAGE

1. Resolves many of the conflicts exemplified in Stage Four.

2. Has a sense of fulfillment regarding personal cultural identity.

3. Increases an appreciation for other cultural groups, as well as dominant cultural values.

4. Selectively accepts or rejects dominant culture values based upon prior experience.

5. Is motivated to eliminate all forms of oppression.

Figure 2
WHITE RACIAL CONSCIOUSNESS MODEL
(Adapted from Helm, 1984)

STAGE ONE
CONTACT STAGE

1. Becomes aware that Black (minority) people exist.

2. Naively characterizes interactions and knowledge about Blacks (minorities).

3. Tends to ignore differences or regard them as unimportant (people are people).

4. Is unaware of self as a racial being (does not know what it means to be White).

5. Becomes aware of societal pressures that accompany cross-racial interactions.

6. Seeks resolution through withdrawal or approach.

STAGE TWO
DISINTEGRATION STAGE

1. Becomes aware of racism, which leads to guilt, depression, and negative feelings. Is forced to acknowledge that he or she is White.

2. Is caught between internal standards of human decency and external cultural expectations.

3. Responds to this dilemma in one of three ways:

   a. Overidentifies with Blacks (minorities).
   b. Becomes paternalistic towards Blacks (minorities).
   c. Retreats back into the White culture.

Figure 2 (Continued)

STAGE THREE
REINTEGRATION STAGE

1. Becomes hostile toward Blacks (minorities) and more positively biased toward own racial group (prejudice).

2. Overtly or covertly becomes anti-Black (minority).

3. Views or perceives Black (minority) traits as negative.

STAGE FOUR
PSEUDO-INDEPENDENT STAGE

1. Intellectually accepts and becomes increasingly curious about Blacks (minorities) and Whites.

2. Becomes interested in racial group similarities/differences.

3. May have cross-racial interactions or may be limited to special Blacks (minorities) (those who are similar to Whites).

STAGE FIVE
AUTONOMY STAGE

1. Accepts racial differences and similarities with appreciation and respect.

2. Does not perceive differences as deficits or similarities as enhancers.

3. Actively seeks opportunities for cross-racial interactions.

Figure 3
GAY AND LESBIAN IDENTITY
DEVELOPMENT MODEL*

STAGE ONE
IDENTITY CONFUSION STAGE

1. Has feelings of turmoil, in which one questions previously held assumptions about one's sexual orientation.

STAGE TWO
IDENTITY COMPARISON STAGE

2. Has feelings of alienation, in which one accepts the possibility of being gay and becomes isolated from non-gay others.

STAGE THREE
IDENTITY TOLERACE STAGE

3. Has feelings of ambivalence, in which one seeks out other gays, but maintains separate public and private images.

STAGE FOUR
IDENTITY ACCEPTANCE STAGE

4. Selectively discloses identity. One begins the legitimization (publicly as well as privately) of one's sexual orientation.

STAGE FIVE
IDENTITY PRIDE STAGE

5. Feels anger, pride, and activism. One becomes immersed in the gay subculture and rejects non-gay people, institutions, and values.

STAGE SIX
IDENTITY SYNTHESIS STAGE

6. Finds clarity and self-acceptance. One moves beyond a dichotomized worldview to an incorporation of one's sexual orientation as one aspect of a more integrated identity.

---

*This summary of Cass (1979) model was included in a recent article by R.E. Fassinger, The Hidden Minority, *Counseling Psychologist*, (1991, April), 167-174.

ACTIVITIES

Self-knowledge is an important first step toward interracial and cross-cultural harmony and communication. Therefore, participants from all ethnic and racial groups must look at themselves seriously and deeply as a prerequisite to dealing with people from other groups. Please try to be as open and as non-defensive as possible when completing these activities.

ACTIVITY 2-1
Minority Identity Development,
White Racial Consciousness Development,
and Gay and Lesbian Identity Development

Objectives

1. To familiarize you with the three models.

2. To help you identify your own level of racial identity or gay identity development.

3. To help you identify the stages of identity development of participants from other racial/ethnic or gay/lesbian backgrounds.

Directions for Participants

1. Minority participants should scan the summary of the *Minority Identity Development Model* (Figure 1), and White participants should scan the *White Racial Consciousness Model* (Figure 2). Gay/lesbian participants should review either Figure 1 or Figure 2 (depending on their racial identification) in addition to Figure 3, *Gay and Lesbian Identity Development Model.*

2. Identify the stage which best describes you.

3. Identify the stage in which you experienced the greatest amount of conflict or confusion.

4. Identify the stage in which you believe personal growth is needed.

Directions for Group Leaders

After participants have completed Items 1 through 4 above, place them in small heterogeneous groups (seven to nine members each) and ask them to discuss the following items:

1. Identify and discuss your stage of identity development.

2. Identify one or two factors or events that contributed to your identification with a particular stage.

3. Identify the stage that caused the greatest amount of conflict for you. Explain.

4. Discuss implications for personal growth.

ACTIVITY 2-2
Reflections of Minority, Majority and Gay/Lesbian Students:
A Look in the Mirror

Objectives

1. To help you understand the evolution of your racial/cultural gay/lesbian attitude development.

2. To help you become aware of your level or stage of racial/cultural gay/lesbian consciousness.

3. To help you determine what, if anything, you would like to do to change your negative racial attitudes or behaviors or non-productive attitudes or feelings about being gay.

Directions for Minority Participants

1. Imagine that you can see reflections, in a mirror, of your life experiences with other culturally or racially different individuals. As you look into this imaginary mirror . . .

   a. Do you see a person who is ashamed of being ethnically or culturally different, and who idealizes the dominant White heterosexual culture?

   b. Do you see a person who is not interested in learning about his/her African, Asian, Hispanic, or Native American ancestry; or about the contributions of Gays and Lesbians to the American Society?

c. Do you see a person who is so immersed in his/her own cultural group that he/she cannot relate to members of the White dominant society?

d. Do you see a person who is confused about loyalty to his/her own cultural group and his/her personal autonomy?

e. Do you see a person who has an appreciation of other cultural and minority groups, as well as an appreciation of his/her own?

f. Do you see a person who is doing his/her part in eliminating all forms of oppression and racial/ethnic/cultural discrimination?

2. Now, think of the image that emerged strongest for you and prepare to discuss your image with others at a later time.

Directions for White Participants

1. Imagine you can see reflections, in a mirror, of your life experiences with individuals whose race, culture, or sexual orientation is different from your own. As you look into this imaginary mirror . . .

    a. Do you see a person who has had little or no contact with Black American, Asian American, Hispanic American, Native American, or Gay/Lesbian people?

    b. Do you see a person who does not know what it means to be in the White majority and the impact of his/her majority status on minority individuals or groups?

    c. Do you see a person who would rather be non-supportive of minorities than to risk being rejected by his/her own peer group?

    d. Do you see a person who believes he/she has to take care of people from minority groups?

e.   Do you see an individual who is covertly or overtly anti-Black, anti-Asian, anti-Hispanic, anti-Native American, or anti-Gay/Lesbian?

f.   Do you see a person who believes that positive cross-cultural relationships are possible only with certain ethnic minority people (those who are most similar to you)?

g.   Do you see a person who accepts cultural and sexual orientation differences and similarities with appreciation and respect?

h.   Do you see a person who supports diversity and actively seeks opportunities to eliminate oppression and to create an open society?

2.   Now, think of the image that emerged strongest for you and prepare to discuss it with others.

Directions for Gay/Lesbian Participants

1. Imagine you can see reflections, in a mirror, of your life experiences with individuals whose sexual orientation is different from your own. As you look into this imaginary mirror . . .

    a. Do you see a person in turmoil concerning earlier assumptions about his/her sexual orientation?

    b. Do you see a person who feels alienated from non-gay people as you accept the possibility of being gay?

    c. Do you see an individual who experiences mixed emotions about being gay and attempts to maintain separate public and private images?

    d. Do you see a person who selectively self-discloses about being gay?

e. Do you see an individual who takes pride in being gay, who immerses in the gay culture, and who actively rejects non-gay individuals?

f. Do you see a person who feels secure in his/her sexual orientation and who has incorporated this orientation as one aspect of his/her total identity?

2. Now, think of the image that emerged strongest for you and prepare to discuss it with others.

Directions for Group Leaders

1. Place participants in small **heterogeneous** groups (seven to nine members each) and direct them to discuss the following questions:

   a. Which image of yourself was most unclear and generated the most doubt for you?

   b. Which image was moderately clear but still questionable for you?

   c. Which image was most clear and understandable for you?

d. What insights did you gain from participating in this activity?

e. Which factor or life experience had the greatest impact on the development of your racial/ethnic/ sexual identity image?

f. What similarities and differences were observed between minority and majority participants?

g. What, if anything, does this activity cause you to want to do?

2. Summarize or ask group members to summarize key points, themes, and any suggestions derived from the group discussion.

ACTIVITY 2-3
In Their Shoes

Objectives

1. To help you understand certain attitudes and feelings of individuals from different racial/cultural groups.

2. To help you acquire knowledge about people from different racial cultural groups.

3. To help you to link concepts of racial/cultural identity with life circumstances.

4. To help you develop greater cross-cultural appreciation.

Directions for Participants

1. Join a homogenous group of five to seven other participants based on their racial/cultural identity. You should have small groups of ethnic minority and small groups of White majority members in separate groups. Gay/lesbian participants should join groups based on their racial/cultural identity.

2. In your small groups, study the characteristics of one of the stages of identity development of the racial/cultural group different from your own. Then, role-play a five-minute vignette reflective of one of the stages. Therefore, White participants will be role-playing minority stages (see Figure 1) and minority students will be role-playing White majority stages (see Figure 2).

3. Use your best estimation about the attitudes and feelings of people in the stage you will be representing, and select members in your groups to reproduce realistic life experiences of the people you are role-playing.

Directions for Group Leaders

1. After each group role-plays one of the stages for the entire group of either the MIDM or the WRCM (Figures 1 and 2), process the group experience by raising the following questions:

    a. On what bases did you select the stage to role-play?

    b. How did each group member feel in his/her different roles?

    c. What knowledge or insight did you gain through your participation in the role-play?

2. After each group has responded to questions about their group participation, ask members to discuss their views and feelings about participants from other cultures role-playing qualities of your racial/cultural group. You may raise the following questions:

    a. How did you feel about individuals from other racial/cultural groups role-playing qualities of your own racial/cultural group?

    b. How accurately did members from other cultural groups portray characteristics of your racial/cultural group?

    c. What is one misconception that other groups often make about your group that you would like to clarify?

    d. Ask members to state what they learned from the total experiment.

ACTIVITY 2-4
Exploring Racial/Cultural Identity Development: A Trip Back

Objectives

1. To help you become more aware of your own racial/ cultural identity development.

2. To help you become more aware of racial/cultural identity attitudes of other students.

3. To help you develop action strategies to progress from one stage to another.

Directions for Participants

1. Each minority student should scan Figure 1 (MID) and each White majority student should scan Figure 2 (WRCM) until you identify the stage that most closely represents your attitudes, perception, and behaviors.

2. Think back over your life history and try to recall some of the factors that may have influenced the development of your racial/cultural identity attitudes.

3. Consider some of the following factors to assist your recall:

    a. Messages you heard from your family about culturally different people.

    b. Portrayal of culturally different people through the media (radio, television, newspapers and advertisement).

    c. Attitudes of your peer group toward culturally different individuals.

d. A positive experience you had with a culturally different person.

e. A negative experience you had with a culturally different person.

f. Attitudes of your parents toward culturally different individuals.

Directions for Group Leaders

1. After each member has had sufficient time to recall factors that influenced his/her racial/cultural development, ask participants to share any part of their recollections about which they would feel comfortable.

2. Ask participants to share what they believe is a linkage between their current racial/cultural attitudes and their experiences.

3. Help participants identify and discuss common themes and life experiences concerning their racial/cultural identity which they all share.

ACTIVITY 2-5
Literary Sharing:
A Vehicle for Multicultural Understanding

Objectives

1. To help you understand the relationship between concepts of racial/cultural identity development and literary characters.

2. To help you expand your awareness and knowledge about racial/cultural identity development through literature and the arts.

Directions for Participants

1. Take a few minutes to think about how racial/cultural identity attitudes and behaviors (MID or WRCM) are manifested in (a) characters in novels you have read; (b) characters in movies you have seen; (c) the life and works of historical characters; (d) the life and works of contemporary characters; (e) characters portrayed in poetry and other literary works, and (f) well- known local, state and national leaders.

2. Discuss the racial/cultural identity attitudes of one or two of these characters with another person in the group. For example, it might be interesting to discuss the evolution of Malcolm X's cultural identification, pointing out his conforming attitudes (processing his hair to resemble that of a White person), his resistance and immersion stage (preaching hate for White people), and his integrative awareness attitudes (where he advocated human rights for all people). You might identify events in the lives of these characters that might have caused them to move from one stage of identity development to another.

Directions for Group Leaders

1. Have participants discuss the identity attitudes of their characters in dyads for 15 minutes. Then ask those in dyads to join others to form groups of four. After 10 minutes of discussion in groups of four, have them join others to form groups of eight—then 16 until the group becomes one large group.

2. Have participants identify and discuss themes that may have emerged concerning their characters. In addition, have them identify and discuss similarities and differences of racial/cultural attitudes among the characters.

3. Now, ask participants to think about what this activity means relative to their feelings about their own racial/cultural identity development. For example, have them explore questions like:

   a. With which character do I most strongly identify?

   b. With which character do I least identify?

   c. In what ways do I want to change with regards to my racial/cultural identity development?

ACTIVITY 2-6
Exploring Our Racial/Cultural Identity Development

Objectives

1. To help you explore and understand your own racial/cultural identity attitudes.

2. To explore and understand the racial/cultural identity development of others.

3. To help you become more aware of the development of your racial/cultural identity development.

Directions for Participants

One way to understand your own racial/cultural identity attitudes is to have a very open and honest discussion about it with another person. Therefore, you and a friend, or a workshop participant, might interview one another using some of the following questions:

1. How was your development similar to and different from the characteristics in the model? (See Figures 1 and 2)

2. How did you resolve conflicts identified in the model?

3. What life experiences or events impacted upon your movement among the various stages?

4. Where do you think you are now regarding your racial/cultural identity development?

5. Are there things you would like to do to enhance your relationship with individuals from culturally different groups?

Directions for Group Leaders

1. Move around among participants as they share and interview one another about their racial/cultural identity development.

2. After 20 to 30 minutes of interpersonal sharing, ask participants to share any insights they have gained with the larger group.

3. Record any themes from individual sharing and use the themes to summarize the activity.

4. Encourage participants to continue to be aware of their racial/cultural identity development and to be willing to change those attitudes that hinder positive multicultural relations.

REFERENCES

Atkinson, D. R., Morten, G., & Sue, D. W. (1979). *Counseling American minorities: A cross-cultural perspective.* Dubuque, IA: W. C. Brown.

Cass, V.C. (1979). Homosexual identity formation: A theoretical model. *Journal of Homosexuality, 4,* 219-235.

Fassinger, R.E. (1991, April). The hidden minority. *Counseling Psychologist,* 167-174.

Helms, J. E. (1984). Toward a theoretical explanation of the effects of race on counseling: A Black and White model. *The Counseling Psychologist, 12*(4), 153-163.

Katz, J.H., & Ivey, A. (1977). White awareness: The frontier of racism awareness training. *Personnel and Guidance Journal, 55*(8), 485-487.

Smith, E. M. J. (1985). Ethnic minorities: Life stress, social support, and mental health issues. *The Counseling Psychologist, 13,* 537-579.

Sue, D. W. (1978). World views and counseling. *Personnel and Guidance Journal, 56,* 485-462.

Chapter **3**

STEREOTYPING

Walter Lippman (1949), a famous journalist, first used the term "stereotype" in his book *Public Opinion*. He defined stereotyping as a kind of oversimplification or overgeneralization, which is an attempt to make the world more understandable and manageable. He discussed the use of stereotyping with racial and ethnic groups, and concluded that it was both irrational and inaccurate because of the simple fact that no general behavior or attitude statements can be true about a large class of people. Sociologists and psychologists at first thought that it would be relatively easy to point out to people the irrationality of their stereotypic thinking, and then persuade them to think more clearly.

BACKGROUND

Of course, this didn't happen. Many studies have been completed over the years that demonstrate how deeply ingrained stereotypes are and how difficult it is to change them. Scientists now realize that stereotyping (attempting to put things in simple categories) is natural for human beings and that it is an essential part of our thinking process. We probably evolved, at least in part, because of our ability to develop language and categories so that we can communicate. The presence of this natural tendency to group things in categories helps explain why so much difficulty has been encountered in getting people to move beyond stereotypes relative to race and other minority status.

Stereotypes are very common in our society and on college campuses. In addition to race, religion, and nationality, an almost infinite number of other group stereotypes exists. We tend to believe certain things about men, about women, about Gays, about Lesbians, about old people, about young people, about fat people, about redheads, about fraternities, about sororities, and on and on. This presents a curious paradox in that most educated people realize the absurdity of making generalizations about large classes of people, yet they often continue to use stereotypes in their own thinking.

Stereotypes persist for several reasons. First, stereotypes are not totally irrational, as was thought previously. People usually do not really believe that *all* members of a particular group have the same characteristics, but they do often believe that members of that group *typically* have those characteristics. Students on college campuses do not really believe that *all* Asian American students are scholars, but many do, in fact, believe that Asian American students are *typically* very smart and achievement-oriented. They do not really believe that all Gay men are promiscuous, but they do believe that Gay men are *typically* promiscuous.

STEREOTYPING PROCESS

By allowing for exceptions, a person who holds stereotypic views can cling to them and yet not feel that he or she is being unfair to all members of a group. This is where we get the phenomenon of, "Some of my best friends are _____." In this situation, an individual defends against changing stereotypes by seeing the group member that they know as being different from others in the group. In other words, that person (the exception) is not typical of the larger group. Somehow people find it rational and acceptable to believe that a characteristic is true of most people in a particular class, rather than to believe that they all have that characteristic. Unfortunately, when the beliefs about most of the people in that class are negative, all of the people in the class suffer from the negative stereotype. For example, one stereotype on campus is that African Americans have trouble with standard English and that they cannot write or speak well. African

American students often report that, because of this belief, professors and other students assume that they are deficient in English. This can have many negative consequences on individual students. They may shy away from careers requiring writing or speaking, start to believe that their abilities are inferior and perform more poorly in class, or get so angry and hurt that their achievement suffers.

One interesting question about stereotypes that remains unanswered is whether stereotypes *reflect* already existing negative attitudes toward particular groups, or whether stereotypes *affect* how groups are treated. For example, are African-Americans stereotyped as lazy, pleasure loving, and ostentatious and are Hispanics characterized as slow and lacking ambition because negative and hostile feelings already exist about them among Whites? Or do these stereotypes and labels that have existed for some time create and increase racial prejudice and discrimination? Quite likely, both occur in a kind of negative cycle. Negative labels create hostility and hostility creates negative labels.

ETHNOCENTRISM

One explanation for the original hostility that seems to generate negative labels and stereotypes in the racial and ethnic areas is ethnocentrism. Clear evidence is available that all humans are ethnocentric; that is, they tend to support their own group above others. A classic social psychology experiment demonstrates this. Researchers divided school boys into two groups for a task of counting dots. One group was called "over-estimators" and one group was called "under-estimators." The boys were then randomly told that they belonged to one group or the other. They were then given a number of points, worth money, to assign to each group. They assigned more of their points to the group to which they thought they belonged. In larger economic terms, the groups in power tend to favor members of their own groups.

OVERCOMING STEREOTYPING

We know, then, that people stereotype and that stereotyping is a natural and explainable phenomenon. We also know that, although people can get beyond stereotypes to make judgments based on their knowledge of an individual, stereotypes often affect the way that judgments are made about people, and various minority groups are often recipients of negative judgment based on negative stereotypes. What is the answer, then, to working past these harmful and difficult-to-break-down stereotypes? Awareness and contact seem to be the keys to overcoming stereotyping.

By becoming *aware* of your own stereotyping process, particularly with regard to minority groups, you have a better chance of overcoming your reliance on stereotyping. Your work in the previous chapter on becoming aware of how you formed your attitudes about various minorities will help here.

Contact is the other key. When you know someone from a particular minority group as a person, you have made the first step in overcoming stereotypes about that person. You have to move beyond considering that person as an exception to the stereotype, however. To say that some of your best friends are Gay or Black or Hispanic is not enough. You have to allow your relationship with an individual, or your knowledge of individuals, to affect the way that you think, feel, behave, and make decisions about people in that group. The following activities will help you confront your own and your campus' stereotypes.

ACTIVITY 3-1
Campus Stereotypes

This activity is designed to encourage participants to identify and discuss stereotypes about minority groups on campus. The first step in confronting stereotypes is to bring them into consciousness and to discuss them openly. A kind of double standard concerning stereotypes on college campuses exists. College students know that stereotypes are socially unacceptable, so they are seldom discussed openly. This is an opportunity to bring campus stereotypes out in the open.

Objectives

1. To identify common campus stereotypes about various minority groups.

2. To confront and challenge these stereotypes.

Directions for Participants

You will be divided into a number of small homogeneous groups. (People from minority groups will be in groups with others of that same minority.) You will need to decide which minority groups are represented among your group and put students together according to those groupings. Majority White students will be put in their own groups. Gay and Lesbian students can choose whether to be in a group based on race/ethnic background or sexual orientation; however, the activity will work better if at least one group represents Gay/Lesbian students.

Each group is to pick out two or three other groups and list the stereotypes that members of their group have of that group. They should act as if representing their entire campus population. For example, White majority students will represent stereotypes held by White students toward other minority campus groups; Black students will represent stereotypes held by campus Black students about White majority and other minority students on campus; and so on. The groups will have about 20 to 30 minutes to list on separate sheets of paper stereotypes for other groups. After that, each group will report their stereotypes to members of the other groups.

Students will then be divided into small heterogeneous groups to discuss their feelings and reactions to the campus stereotypes identified.

Directions for Group Leaders

The most important part of this exercise is the final step when students discuss the stereotypes and try to understand how these stereotypes were formed and how they affect the victims of the stereotypes. Each group should be given the following list of discussion questions, and leaders should be on the lookout for potential conflict or negative reactions. These conflicts are not necessarily bad, but they need to be brought out into the open and discussed. Having trained group leaders to supervise this final step would be helpful. Following are examples of questions to be discussed in these groups:

1. How did you feel listing the stereotypes?

2. How did you feel when the stereotypes were read out in front of the large group?

3. How do you think that the negative stereotypes about your group affect you and others in that group?

4. Do you feel that there is any truth to the stereotypes?

5. How do the stereotypes become institutionalized at your school; i.e., do they affect school policies, student government, the fraternity/sorority system, etc.?

6. Do you think that more interaction would break down these stereotypes?

7. How do you fight your own tendency to use these stereotypes in your thinking and judging?

ACTIVITY 3-2
Labels

In this activity, participants learn about labels and how destructive they can be. Label cards, about 3 inches by 14 inches, will be made with various group labels printed on them. Each end will be attached to a string about 18 inches long, so that the string can be placed around the participant's neck with the label hanging on his or her back. A label will be placed on each participant's back, without the participant knowing which label he or she gets. After everyone gets a label, the large group is instructed to mill around and try to talk with as many other people as possible. No one is to identify people's labels to them. In the course of conversation, each person is to make some comment to the other person that indicates one of the stereotypic assumptions commonly made about the group whose label the person is wearing on his or her back. Following are some examples:

> **Hispanic**—It must be hard to learn English when all you people talk at home is Spanish.

> **Jew**—You people are so good at business. It must be nice to have so much money.

> **Women's Libber**—Why is it you women all hate men? Are you Lesbians?

> **Gay**—Isn't it hard to control yourself when you want to have sex with every guy you see?

> **Fraternity Boy**—How do you guys get through school when all you do is drink and party?

After about 20 minutes, you will be asked to break up into small groups to discuss your reactions to this exercise.

Objectives

1. To experience how labeling and having assumptions made about one based on stereotypes makes one feel.

2. To experience what verbalizing ridiculous negative stereotypes is like.

3. To explore feelings and attitudes about campus stereotypes.

Directions for Participants

This may seem difficult at first. Try to be creative and come up with statements showing stereotypic assumptions about each group. Remember that the activity is not meant to be realistic. People seldom come up to groups and make these kinds of stupid comments. However, you would probably be surprised at the number of times people do make comments similar to these. Don't worry about being subtle. Remember that these aren't comments that you necessarily believe. You are doing this to help each other experience what having a label is like.

In the discussion afterwards, try to use your imagination to see what you might feel like if you really were a person with that label on your campus. Try to really feel what it might be like.

Directions for Group Leaders

You will need to help structure this activity. Make certain that everyone understands the directions and that participants mill around and talk to several people. You can call, "Switch!" periodically, if necessary. You will need to prepare the labels ahead of time. Pick out a good representation of labels from your campus and use the pejorative terms. Following are some suggested labels:

Queer	Fag	Lesbo
Nigger	Jungle Bunny	Kike
Blond Airhead	Jew	Gook
Dumb Jock	Joe Stud	Frat Boy
JAP	Libber	Maneater
Spick	Taco Eater	Dorm Rat

You may need to consult with a group of students to ascertain labels used on your campus.

For the small group discussion, participants should be put in heterogeneous groups. The groups should discuss the following questions:

1. What kind of questions did the different labels elicit?

2. What was it like to have the label? How did you feel?

3. How long before you guessed your label?

4. What was it like to ask the questions based on negative stereotypes?

5. Which labels seemed to evoke the most negative stereotypes?

6. Did differences exist among kinds of labels; i.e., race, ethnic origin, sexual orientation, type of behavior, etc.?

After the small group discussions, bring the group back and ask each small group to share one important comment or realization that came out of their discussion.

ACTIVITY 3-3
Major Campus Stereotypes

Small heterogeneous groups have the task of identifying five major stereotypes about each of the major minority groups on campus (i.e., Gays are promiscuous, Asians are smart, etc.). They are then asked to identify at least two harmful effects for each stereotype. They then report the stereotyping and harmful effects back to the large group.

Objectives

1. To encourage open discussion of stereotypes.

2. To increase awareness of the process of stereotyping and its potential harm.

3. To increase empathy for victims of stereotyping.

Directions for Participants

At first identifying harmful stereotypes may be difficult, particularly since you are in a group that may include members of the groups for which you are discussing and identifying major stereotypes. Remember that the purpose of this activity is to increase your awareness and to demonstrate the harmful and offensive nature of stereotyping.

Directions for Group Leaders

The hardest part of this activity for the groups will be getting started. You may need to help some of the groups who are having trouble being honest about stereotypes. You also will need to monitor time for this activity. Groups should be asked to complete the initial task in 20 to 30 minutes. The small group should report back to the larger group. The discussion should focus on the negative effects of stereotyping.

ACTIVITY 3-4
Personal Stereotyping

This is a short activity that focuses on personal stereotyping. Students will examine their own lives and discuss in small groups their reactions to being stereotyped.

Objectives

1. To increase awareness and understanding of the stereotyping process and negative effects.

2. To increase empathy for victims of stereotyping.

Directions for Participants

Some concentrated thinking may be needed for some of you to remember times when you were stereotyped. You will need to think broadly here. Don't just think about stereotypes because of race or culture. Perhaps you were stereotyped because you are male or female, because you are thin or heavy, because you came from a poor or a wealthy family, or perhaps because you wear glasses or belong to the chess club! Discuss in small groups the stereotypes that you have encountered. Did anyone else come up with the same or similar ones? Discuss with your small group your feelings and reactions to being stereotyped.

Directions for Group Leaders

Some participants may have trouble coming up with memories of being stereotyped. To help them, give examples and have them think back to childhood experiences. If someone can't think of any, they can still learn by participating in the small group discussion. After the small group discussion, which should last 15 to 20 minutes, convene the entire group and get some feedback from each group about how the activity worked.

REFERENCE

Lippman, W. (1949). *Public Opinion.* New York: Macmillan.

Chapter **4**

EMPATHY AND AWARENESS OF CAMPUS MINORITIES

One way to break stereotypes is to better understand how different minority students experience campus life. By developing empathy and understanding for different campus minorities, you will be less likely to stereotype groups because of lack of knowledge. Developing this empathy is another important step in making progress toward becoming a culturally effective person.

The purpose of this chapter is to identify and discuss experiences and perceptions of selected minority group students. This will help you gain a better understanding and appreciation of their view of the world as they see it and live it on college campuses. The groups selected offer unique and special insights into their experiences as well as common and shared experiences of minorities on campuses. African-American students, Jewish students, Hispanic students, Asian-American students, and Lesbian and Gay students will be discussed.

AFRICAN-AMERICAN STUDENTS

The experiences and perceptions of African-American students on predominantly White campuses have been subject to numerous studies and research projects over the past twenty-five years. While some things have changed for the better, many problems still exist. Beckham (1987-88) wrote:

> African-American students have the same needs as all humankind. They deserve a sustained sense of self-worth and self-esteem and the encouraging support of faculty, administrators and student peers. Academically and psychologically, the critical issue for all students is that of surviving to achieve. Repeatedly, however, Black experiences in mostly White colleges are chronicles of how institutions have systematically bruised self-esteem.

Beckham's assertion is supported by the following comments of selected African-American students who participated in a survey conducted by the Southern Regional Educational Board (Abraham, 1990):

1. My school has a policy of good race relations that it does not follow through with. We (Black students) seem to be tolerated—not really accepted. In response, Black students become distant with each other in an effort not to appear too different. It's sad.

2. Black students on a predominantly White campus seem to have to do more to prove themselves worthy. The faculty is not as willing to help us as they are to help our (White) counterparts. This school is becoming more and more integrated but this isn't the will of the overall school.

3. I have found that the White students keep to themselves. They really don't want to be social. The students harbor all the stereotypical prejudices. I think what (the institution) needs is a course or event that makes it mandatory for people of opposite races to socialize together. Whenever there are school events, they are generally geared to the interests of all the White students or all the Black students.

4. I feel that the lack of knowledge White students have about African-Americans hinders their ability to accept us as equals on my college campus.

5. Racial remarks seem to go unchecked. Financial aid is imperative for most Blacks, but academic standards should never be lowered. Instead, make tutoring available.

6. I would like to add that Black students are not looking for special attention from faculty and administrators, just equal opportunity for advancement in life.

7. The fact that (a college trustee) keeps making racial slurs in public and is still on the Board deeply troubles me. How obvious does racism have to be before the proper actions are taken?

According to the SREB (Abraham, 1990), these statements were typical of comments of many of the students represented in their survey. Other surveys and studies have provided similar insight. Note the following personal account of a classroom experience by a Black student that appears in *Black Issues in Higher Education* (August 16, 1990, p.6, Judy Tachibana):

> Right now, I am dealing with a professor and I'm having a lot of racial problems with him. It is hard to walk into a classroom every day and know that this man has a grudge against me because of my color. If I raise my hand to respond to a question he asks or to make a comment, he does anything he can to avoid me. When I started sitting in the front, he would just walk beyond me and give me the little eye look. Just recently in class, I asked a simple question about an experiment that we were doing and he implied that I was stupid for asking the question. From talking with other Black students who have had him in the past, they say that they've had problems and they've confronted him. His comment to me and to them is, "Don't take it personally." "Well, what am I supposed to do? I don't care how much you don't like me, the main reason I'm in the classroom is to learn."

Another Black student in discussing her experiences at a predominantly White institution reported:

> Black students feel like they always have to prove themselves to other people on campus. Many White students and faculty seem to think we are here only because of affirmative action, admissions quotas and special programs. While some Black students might be admitted because of special programs, not all of us are. The one thing that disturbs me a great deal is the assumption that I don't belong here and that I only got in because of my color and not my ability.

Concern about the lack of Black faculty and administrators was expressed by one student as follows:

> In my three years at the University, I have only had one Black professor. There are no Black faculty members in my department. It seems that the university does not see the importance of having Black faculty members—not only as role models for Black students but for White students as well.

While it would not be fair to assume that the aforementioned comments and perceptions reported are representative of all Black students at all predominantly White institutions, they are indeed reality for many students. Concern about relationships with White students and faculty members, feelings of isolation and alienation, and a general sense of being "unwelcomed" appear to be quite common. Moreover, recognizing the concern expressed by Black students that they are often viewed as products of affirmative action programs and admissions quotas is important in order to understand the feelings of Black students attending predominantly White schools. Being aware of the effect on Black students of having few role models in predominantly White institutions is also crucial to an understanding of how these Black students feel.

JEWISH STUDENTS

A recent report by the Anti-Defamation League (ADL) indicated that Jewish students have been the subject of increased anti-Semitic incidents. Johnston (1991) reported that hate crimes against Jews rose to a record level in 1990. Citing the results of a nationwide survey by the ADL, he noted that incidents against Jews rose for the fourth straight year. Johnston goes on to state that the report notes a "particularly troubling" increase of bias-related incidents on college campuses. "Anti-Semitic and racist attacks are particularly troubling when they occur in a university environment devoted to respect for diverse ideas, people and cultures," said A. H. Foxman, the League's National Spokesman (Johnston, 1991, p. 2). David Freedman (1991), Director of the League's Washington office, commented that the increase in campus hate crimes reflected both growing bigotry among young people and a greater willingness among victims to report the crimes (*Chronicle of Higher Education*, February 13, 1991, p.2).

As Freedman suggested, incidents of harassment, vandalism, and violence continue to be of concern to many Jewish students on college and university campuses. These concerns are supported by comments given by the following Jewish students interviewed regarding their personal experiences.

Jill, a public relations major, reported:

> Last year, someone painted swastikas and other degrading graffiti on the walls of the Jewish Student Center. This incident not only made me very angry but frightened me a great deal. I couldn't believe that there were people who hated Jews so much that they would vandalize our Center.

David, a second-year residence hall student, gave this account of an incident in which he was involved:

> One night, while studying in my room with my door open, a group of male residents who had obviously been drinking walked by my room. I heard one of them loudly say, "Looks like Jew boy stayed in tonight to study." I was really upset but I was afraid to confront them.
>
> I thought about reporting the incident to my R.A., but I felt that nothing would happen, so why go through the hassle. A few days later, I told a group of my Jewish friends about this incident and they said that I should have reported the incident to my R.A. They all felt that by my not reporting the incident it would only encourage this group to continue their anti-Semitic slurs.

While many Jewish students are able to assimilate into campus life activities, doing so is not without difficulty. Note the comments from Robin, an active student leader:

> Being actively involved in student activities and student organizations, I have discovered a lot of ignorance about Jewish culture by other students, particularly during high holiday times. Meetings are scheduled and major events are planned with little or no thought about the Jewish holy days. To me and other Jewish students, this shows a lack of respect for our religion and culture.

Another Jewish student reported the following interaction in a classroom situation:

> One of the things that has really upset me and a lot of other Jewish students is when faculty members give major assignments that conflict with our high holy days. It seems like every year I have had a professor who would make some classroom assignment that conflicts with our high holidays. So I have had to go and explain to them about our holiday and ask for a make-up exam or permission to turn in my assignment after the deadline. While all of the professors have cooperated, I wish I didn't have to explain this all the time.

HISPANIC STUDENTS

According to Fields (1988), Hispanic students made up approximately 8.2% of the entire 18-to 24-year-old population in 1985; however, they accounted for only 3.1% of the enrollment at four-year colleges and 6.4% of that at two-year colleges. In addition to being underrepresented, Hispanic students' concerns about their college experiences commonly focus on the following issues:

1. Ignorance of other students about Hispanic cultures.

2. A feeling of loneliness and tension in a different culture.

3. A lack of Hispanic faculty and staff role models.

4. Difficulty in breaking family ties.

5. Language difficulties.

Fiske (1988), in an article entitled "The Undergraduate Hispanic Experience," wrote:

> For many Hispanic students, the most serious problems are not those they confront getting into college but those

they face once they get there. Those problems range from the anxiety of breaking close family ties, to loneliness and tensions inherent in finding their way in institutions built around an alien culture. Some Hispanic undergraduates complain of subtle or not-so-subtle discrimination. Even those from secure and privileged backgrounds are often thrown off balance by finding themselves identified as belonging to a "minority" group for the first time.

Fiske's assertions about the Hispanic student experiences are supported by the following excerpts from interviews with selected students.

Maria, a 19-year-old second-year student, reported:

After being admitted to the University and attending the university's orientation program, I received a letter inviting me to participate in what was called the university's "Minority Student Mentor Program." I had never really thought of myself as a minority before. According to the letter, this mentor program was supposed to be for Black and Hispanic students during their first year at school and would include a faculty mentor who would provide support and be a resource for me during my first year at the university. The program sounded great but I wondered why it was called the "minority" student program and why I was invited to participate as I never view myself as a minority.

Juan, a third-year engineering student, reported:

I had to make a difficult decision about attending this school. I come from a large family and we are all very close. Being the oldest child and the first to go to college, it was difficult to leave home. Many of my friends decided to stay at home and attend the local community college but I had a scholarship offer and really wanted to attend the State University. During my first year at school, I was really homesick and took advantage of every opportunity to go home on the weekends. Because I did this, I never really got involved in campus life activities like other students. While I felt like I was missing out on some things, the need to go home and be with my family was more important.

Gloria, a Hispanic female in psychology, gave the following account:

For many Hispanic students, English is a difficult language. Many of us never speak English at home. While some students are fluent in English and Spanish, many are not. On several occasions, I have observed White students laughing at Hispanic students speaking out in class discussions. They make fun of the broken English spoken by some Hispanic students and do not realize the embarrassment this causes. It really makes me angry when other students make fun of the way my fellow Hispanic students speak.

Alberto, a third-year liberal arts major, reported:

The high school I attended had a Hispanic principal and a large number of teachers were Hispanic. Since being at the University, I've seen very few Hispanic administrators and I have had only one Hispanic teacher for a class. Several of my Black friends say that same thing about the lack of Black faculty and administrators. It seems like the University wants Hispanic and Black students to attend the university but they don't realize how important it is to have role models for us.

ASIAN-AMERICAN STUDENTS

Hsia (1988) reported that Asian-Americans comprise about 2% of the national population but earn about 2.6% of all bachelor's degrees, 2.78% of master's degrees and 3.4% of doctoral degrees every year. Nationally, about 9 out of 10 Asian-American high school graduates attend some form of post-secondary education institution. The academic success of Asian-Americans can be attributed to hard work and a high level of dedication to achievement. As Saigo (1988) wrote: "In the Asian world, family pride, academic achievement, hard work and effort to succeed have high priorities." All too often, however, the success of Asian-American students is perceived to be related to some "natural" ability rather than hard work and industry. Consequently, many Asian-American students are frequently typecast as the "model minority," fueled by myths and stereotypes. Note this comment from an Asian-American student:

A lot of things that shouldn't have anything to do with race get racial labels . . . If someone does well at school, it's not because they're Asian but because they study hard and take it seriously. (Magner, 1990, p. A37)

Asian-American students are also subject to incidents of overt and covert racism as well. Note the following account from one Korean student as reported by Nancy Ramsey (1990):

Once she was leaving a party with another Korean friend when a few drunken male students called out, "Those Chinks are coming out now." We walked past them and it hit me, they were talking about us . . . I was angry but too shocked to know what to do.

Another time, she was talking with friends when a young man came into the room, saw her and said, "Chop Suey, huh?" Everyone looked at him blankly so he repeated it. There was this uncomfortable silence until he left. I was in shock. Later, I felt really angry. When I first went to school I thought it would be a place where everybody was open-minded and intelligent. It was a big surprise to find ignorance and racism.

Another Asian-American reported the following encounter with his faculty adviser:

During my first semester at school I made an appointment to see an academic adviser. I walked into his office and he seemed to automatically assume that I was interested in math or science. Upon telling him that I was interested in fine arts, he expressed surprise. I felt like he wanted me to defend why I was interested in fine arts and not science or math, and this really made me angry.

LESBIAN AND GAY STUDENTS

In a recent study of the experiences of women and men students who were Lesbian, Gay, and bisexual (D'Augelli, 1989), the following findings were reported:

1. Nearly three-quarters reported verbal insults directed at them, and nearly 25% reported being threatened with physical violence.

2. Most (94%) did not report victimization to authorities, generally because they feared additional harassment or did not expect any action to follow a complaint.

3. More than one-half reported they were occasionally afraid for their personal safety and over one-third changed their daily routine to avoid harassment.

The above findings are consistent with an earlier study by Herek (1986) involving 200 Gay and Lesbian students at Yale University. According to this research, nearly 50% reported that they had experienced some kind of anti-Gay harassment, and a majority of the students surveyed said they feared for their safety on campus because of the threat of violence.

The experiences of Lesbian and Gay students on college campuses are frequently marked by hostility, harassment, misunderstanding, discrimination, and, in some instances, violence, directly related to their sexual orientation. For some students, trying to hide their homosexuality causes great anxiety and is often stressful and a source of frustration. Note the following excerpts from interviews with Lesbian and Gay students:

Bob, a Junior engineering student, reported:

> I have to be one person on campus and another person off campus. For example, my department recently had a Christmas party for students and faculty. The invitation I received stated that we should bring our girlfriends or spouses with us to the party. I did not feel comfortable bringing my lover so I just did not attend. As always, I felt like I really missed out on a great opportunity to have fun and interact with my fellow students and faculty in my department.

Julie, a lesbian, gave this account:

> In one of my classes, our instructor suggested that we form study groups to help prepare for exams. I joined a group with five other students because I thought it would be a good way to study for tests. My group decided that

we would take turns hosting the study sessions at each of our apartments. As my turn to have the study group at my apartment neared, I became fearful. How would the other students react to seeing pictures of me and my lover? What about the books and magazines I have around my apartment? I could take the pictures down and hide my books and magazines but I did not feel that I should have to do that. When my turn came to have the study group at my apartment, I called everyone and told them I was sick and that the group would have to meet some place else. The next week, I dropped out of the study group.

Another gay student, Paul, talked about his experience pledging a fraternity:

> When I was pledging a fraternity, my pledge class often had informal rap sessions at the fraternity house. Usually, we talked about all kinds of things like religion, politics, etc. Frequently, members of the pledge class would tell jokes which were all too often directed at Blacks, Jews, or Gays. Everyone would laugh, except me. Once, after someone told a story degrading homosexuals, I remember being asked, "Do you like those fags?" I felt terrible but did not have the courage to say anything about it. For me, nothing is worse than feeling that you have to hide who you are.

For other students who are open about their homosexuality, their problems are similar but sometimes different. Note this comment from one Gay student:

> For those of us who are gay and openly acknowledge our homosexuality, we often feel that our interaction with faculty and other students is limited. Our ability to network, participate in study groups, or to take part in social activities with other students is difficult. While it is not true with all people, a lot of people are still very uncomfortable being around homosexuals. And for some people, there is a real fear that we might want to seduce them or somehow, if they are around us, they will catch AIDS.

Homophobia, defined as an irrational fear of homosexuals, is often expressed in various forms of Gay-bashing including violence. Bendel (1986) gave the following accounts:

> In 1984, a student at a midwest state university distributed T-shirts emblazoned with the slogan,

FAGBUSTERS. At this same university, a Gay student barely avoided major injury when he suddenly lost a wheel while driving his car. Upon inspection, the student found that the lug nuts had been loosened. After that, he started receiving phone calls threatening his life. When he complained to the police, they told him it would take some time before they could get to this case. He dropped out of school, and told a friend, "Somebody's trying to kill me and nobody cares."

At a northeastern university, a group of students initiated a "Heterosexuals Fight Back" rally. They also tried to get finals week designated as "Hang a Homo Week" and put up posters that read, "The GAYBUSTERS are coming."

These incidents and others contribute to hostile environments on college and university campuses for Gay and Lesbian students. The themes of isolation, ignorance, harassment, fear, and, in some instances, violence characterize the experiences of many homosexual students in their daily lives. Moreover, Lesbian and Gay students often feel that their interaction with other students and ability to network with faculty and other university personnel is often limited directly because of their sexual orientation. The negative implications associated with these limitations seriously impact the academic and social opportunities for homosexuals in what they perceive to be an atmosphere in which they feel "unwelcome" or uninvited.

Although these examples of different student perceptions are representative and not comprehensive, hopefully they will help you gain some new insights into what life is like for these different groups on college campuses.

ACTIVITIES

The following learning activities, from Wittmer and Scott (1990), are suggested as ways to increase empathy and awareness of campus minorities. These activities provide participants with opportunities to simulate the unique experiences of campus minorities in a structural format and the opportunity to explore and discuss problems and issues from a minority perspective.

ACTIVITY 4-1
Dear Abby

Objectives

1. To provide participants with an understanding of the problems experienced by different campus minority groups.

2. To help students identify and develop solutions to problems and unique situations with which campus minorities have to cope.

Directions for Participants

1. Group participants are asked to divide into groups representing their unique ethnic, cultural, or social orientation; e.g., Black, Hispanic, White, Asian-American, Gay/Lesbian, etc.

2. After appointing a group spokesperson and recorder, each group is asked to develop a statement in letter format which describes a particular problem unique to their minority group on campus.

3. The letter (statement of the problem) should be addressed to "Dear Abby" and ask for advice as to how the problem identified might best be handled or resolved. The letter should be signed according to the nature of the problem presented; e.g., "upset," "forlorn," "left out," "angry," etc.

Directions for Group Leaders

1. After the letters to Dear Abby have been written, they should be collected by the group leaders.

2. A fishbowl-type discussion group format should be set up with chairs placed in a circle and space for participants to surround the participants sitting in the chairs.

3. Each of the groups should be given one of the Dear Abby problems (not their own).

4. Each group is then given the opportunity to sit in the circle. The spokesperson for the group is instructed to read the problem (letter) and the group members offer advice and suggestions on how to solve the specific problems identified.

5. At the end of the discussion of the topic (a 10-minute time limit should be set), time is provided for members of the other groups to offer their comments and thoughts on how the problem can be resolved. (A time limit of 5 minutes is suggested for this part of the activity.)

6. The process is repeated until each group has had an opportunity to respond to a problem.

Two examples of Dear Abby letters are provided.

Dear Abby:

For many Hispanic students, English is a difficult language. Many of us never speak English at home. I have observed on several occasions White students laughing at me and the way I talk in class discussions. This really makes me angry. Should I say something to these students or just ignore them?

Signed "Upset"

Dear Abby:

I am Jewish and I am very involved in student activities on campus. A number of the organizations to which I belong often schedule meetings and programs on Saturdays, which is the Sabbath for Jewish people. Because of my commitment to my religion, I miss out on a great deal of the activities scheduled on Saturdays. I do not understand why some of these programs could not be planned on Sunday or other days of the week. I want to discuss this concern with some of the other campus leaders. Do you have suggestions on how I should approach this issue?

Signed "Missing Out"

ACTIVITY 4-2
Childhood Messages

Objectives

1. To provide you with an opportunity to share how parents, friends and the media (TV and movies) influence your perceptions of others during your childhood years (5 to 15 years of age).

2. To provide you with an opportunity to discuss the messages you give to others about different groups of people.

Directions for Participants

1. Participants are placed into heterogeneous groups by race, sex, religion, etc., with 5-8 persons in each group.

2. Make up a childhood message chart as illustrated in Figure 4. List each of the groups as shown in Figure 4, and then record the childhood messages that you received about each group from the following categories: Parents, Movies, and Friends. Also list the messages that you give others about each group.

Directions for Group Leaders

1. After each group participant has completed the childhood messages chart, group leaders should ask each participant to share two of the childhood messages they received about a particular group of people. Group leaders should lead and encourage discussion within the group focusing on stereotypes, accuracy of perceptions, and the overall impact of parents, friends, and the media on our feelings and thoughts about others.

Figure 4
CHILDHOOD MESSAGE CHART

Group	Childhood Message Received From			Message Given by You to Others
	Parents	Movies	Friends	
American Indians				
Muslims				
Asian Americans				
People with Physical Handicaps				
U.S. Blacks				
Catholics				
Hispanics				
White Anglo Saxon				
Gays and Lesbians				
Non U.S. Blacks				

ACTIVITY 4-3
Pick Your Corner

Objectives

1. To stimulate discussion and the sharing of personal views on specific issues related to diversity and different groups of people.

Directions for Participants

1. Participants are assembled in a large room with open space which is divided into five areas and labeled with large signs as follows:

STRONGLY AGREE
AGREE
DISAGREE
STRONGLY DISAGREE
UNDECIDED

Directions for Group Leaders

1. The group leader reads a statement (see attached statement list), and participants are requested to walk to the corner or area of the room that best describes their beliefs and personal views on the statement.

2. Each group is given five minutes to discuss why they agreed, disagreed, strongly agreed, strongly disagreed, or are undecided on a statement, and what behaviors they have experienced or witnessed that influenced their position on the statement. Participants who are undecided must move to one of the other groups after their discussion period is completed.

3. This process is repeated until all the statements have been read.

4. At the conclusion of this activity, the group leader reviews the group process and discusses those statements that seem to provoke the greatest agreements and those that suggest the greatest disagreements.

PICK YOUR CORNER: ISSUE STATEMENTS

1. Our University is making progress in eliminating racial tensions on campus.

2. Appreciation for diversity is encouraged on our campus by student leaders.

3. Openness and trust characterize communication between Black and White students on our campus.

4. Lesbian and Gay students are openly discriminated against on our campus.

5. Fraternities and sororities on our campus do little to encourage integration of the Greek system at our school.

REFERENCES

Abraham, A. (1990). Racial issues on campus: How students view them. Atlanta, GA: *Southern Regional Educational Board.*

Beckham, B. (Fall 1987-Winter 1988). Strangers in a strange land: The experiences of Blacks on White campuses. *Educational Record,* 75-76.

Bendel, P. (1986, August-September). Hostile eyes. *Campus Voice, 34.*

D'Augelli, A. R. (1989). Lesbian and gay men's experiences of discrimination and harassment in a university community. *American Journal of Community Psychology, 17,* 317-321.

Fields, C. (1988, May-June). The Hispanic pipeline. *Change,* 25.

Fiske, E. (1988, May-June). The undergraduate Hispanic experience. *Change,* 29.

Freedman, D. (1991, February 13). *Chronicle of Higher Education,* 2.

Herek, G., as reported by Bendel, P. (1986). Hostile eyes. *Campus Voice,* 32.

Hsia, J. (1988). *Asian Americans in higher education and at work,* Chapter 5. Hillsdale, NJ: Erlbaum Associates.

Johnston, D. (1991, February 7). Hate crimes reach record high in '90. *Gainesville Sun,* 2.

Magner, D. (1990. November 14). *Chronicle of Higher Education,* A37.

Ramsey, N. (1990, November-December). Divided we stand. *In View,* 10.

Saigo, R. (1989, November-December). The barriers of racism. *Change,* 10.

Tachibana, J. (1990, August 16). Campus climate often hostile to women, minorities, report shows. *Black Issues in Higher Education,* 6.

Wittmer, J. & Scott, J. (1990). A Black/White two day student retreat: The Florida model. ERIC Clearinghouse on Counseling and Personnel Services, CG 022823.

Chapter **5**

BECOMING A CULTURALLY EFFECTIVE PERSON: DEVELOPING SENSITIVITY

One of the goals of a college or university is to provide a diversified environment where students can learn to live effectively with all types of people from all types of cultural backgrounds. If students learn to appreciate, accept, and interact with fellow students on a diversified campus, they will increase their potential toward becoming culturally effective persons (CEP's). Dick Gregory, comedian and longtime civil rights activist stressed the importance of the college environment when he said that college students need to learn more from their college experience than how to make a living. They also need to learn how to *live*. One important aspect of learning how to "live" is learning how to be a culturally effective person.

Several writers have described CEP's. Janet Helms (1984), a noted researcher, suggested that CEP's do not perceive differences among groups of people as deficits, and do not view similarities among them as enhancers. Atkinson, Morten, and Sue (1979), leaders in the field of multicultural counseling, viewed the CEP as one who has achieved a sense of fulfillment regarding personal cultural identity, coupled with an increased appreciation of other ethnic/cultural groups as well as dominant culture values. As we have already pointed out, people in the 1990s will be living in an increasingly multicultural world, and anyone who hopes to be successful will need to be more accepting, flexible, and cross-culturally intelligent.

Most university environments are diverse enough to foster the development of culturally effective persons, and most students have the potential to become CEP's. However, a variety of inhibiting forces block the development of CEP's. Similarly, many factors stimulate the development of CEP's.

INHIBITING FORCES

The major inhibiting factors that exist on most predominantly White college campuses are (1) cultural values, (2) racial/ethnic identity attitudes, (3) negative perceptions and experiences, (4) perceived preferential treatment, and (5) homophobia.

Cultural Values

Class, socioeconomic level, and culture-bound values are impediments to multicultural relations in general and, in particular, to the development of cultural sensitivity among various groups on college campuses. Most White/majority students are from middle-class backgrounds, while minority students are usually from lower-class economic backgrounds. White/majority students and ethnic minority students often come to the university from very different backgrounds, causing each to have different beliefs, skills, values, customs, and language.

Given these differences, one can more easily understand why many White and minority students experience difficulty in relating to and understanding one another. For example, many White/majority students may not be aware of the depth and breadth of problems many of their ethnic minority counterparts experience. They may not be aware of the amount of stress that many minority students feel as a result of worrying about academic survival or about conditions of their impoverished families back home. Their middle-class backgrounds may not allow them to understand the day-to-day financial struggles that many minority students encounter. On the other hand, many minority students may assume that all White/majority students are well-off, when, in fact, some majority students also struggle financially in their pursuit of higher education.

A clear expectation exists for most middle-class White/majority students that they *will* go to college after high school. Unlike many of their ethnic minority counterparts, most are also expected to succeed in college. In addition, these White/majority students are usually admitted through regular admissions criteria and standards. They are often unaware of the psychological consequences for African-American and other minority students of being the first of their families to attend college, and of being admitted to universities on a conditional basis because they often do not qualify under regular admission standards.

Recently, a young White college student reported that she did not understand why Black students congregated on one segment of the campus. She also could not understand why they were so noisy and unfriendly to other students. She did not understand the cultural value for African-American students of being together and having fun, nor did she realize the security needs that brought these students together.

Another White student could not understand why the Asian students in his engineering class were so compliant, subdued, and academically oriented. He assumed that none of them would be very good friends because they probably never had any fun. He did not really understand that showing respect, being reserved, and achieving academically are important values in many Asian cultures.

A Black student could not understand how the White/majority students on his residence hall floor could enjoy the social events that they organized, and the music they listened to seemed totally absurd to him. He could not imagine being friendly with any of them; they seemed to him to be from a different planet. This is another example of misunderstanding and the failure to appreciate different cultural values.

These are just a few examples of cultural values and practices that may be misunderstood and that hinder the development of culturally sensitive attitudes and behaviors. One of the greatest obstacles to becoming a CEP is the challenge of identifying and releasing yourself from the powerful grip of class and culture. *An important step toward change is to become aware of the impact of class and culture on your attitudes and relationships.*

Racial/Ethnic Identity Attitudes

Certain racial attitudes and experiences are barriers to multicultural sensitivity and to cultural effectiveness. "Racial prejudice," defined by Brislin, Cushner, Cherrie, and Young (1986) as negative reactions toward others based on emotions, without direct contact or facts about others, is a core problem. They outlined five forms of prejudice that seem to prevail on college campuses.

1. Red-neck Racism. This is the belief held by certain groups that a given ethnic group is inferior according to imagined standards and that those group members do not deserve decent treatment. This extreme form of racism had its origin in the southern United States, where historically a particular superior/ inferior relationship occurred between Whites and Blacks.

2. Symbolic Racism. One group may have negative feelings about another group because they believe the other group is interfering with certain aspects of their culture. In addition, the other group may be competing for some of the same resources that have been available to the first group. For example, increasing tension occurs between African-Americans and Cuban-Americans because many members from both groups are competing for the same jobs, scholarships, and other economic opportunities.

3. Tokenism. Some individuals hide their true feelings toward other groups by engaging in some insignificant token activity. Through such engagement (e.g., inviting a minority to dinner or picking one minority member for a group), individuals tell themselves they are not prejudiced. Tokenism prevents individuals from participation in more significant or meaningful activities with other groups. For example, some departments on college campuses hire one minority faculty member to satisfy affirmative action guidelines but do not really work to understand minority student and faculty needs.

4. Arm's-length Prejudice. Some people are friendly and kind toward out-group members in certain situations but hold them at arm's length in other situations. An African-American woman reported strong feelings of disappointment toward a White coworker who was friendly at work but ignored her in the grocery store or in other public places. Some minority athletes have given accounts of unity with White players on the field but arm's-length relations off the field.

5. Real Likes and Dislikes. Certain groups hold negative feelings toward others because of particular behaviors. Negative feelings may be held toward those groups they believe have low educational values, have misplaced economic values (e.g., driving expensive cars), are greedy and competitive, or are flamboyant in athletic events (e.g., slam-dunking the basketball or spiking the football after each touchdown).

Social scientists have explored attitudes of Whites toward minorities (Helms, 1984) and minorities toward Whites (Atkinson, Morten, & Sue, 1979). Helms (1984) described certain White college students who do not progress toward becoming more culturally effective. They are naive about racial issues, do not see themselves as "racial beings," and assume that racial differences are individual concerns rather than social or political issues. They believe that affirmative action should not be used to achieve racial balance, nor should special programs be used to address ethnic minority concerns.

Atkinson, Morten, and Sue (1979) also described attitudes and behaviors that contribute to ethnic minority persons being less culturally effective. For such students, identity and worth are defined by the White/majority group. They are ashamed of their own ethnic heritage, and have very little knowledge of the positive aspects of their histories and the contributions they have made toward the development of this country.

Negative Perceptions and Experiences

Negative perceptions and negative experiences between majority and minority students are major barriers to cultural effectiveness among students. When one considers the fact that ethnic minorities have historically been described negatively in all types of literature, one can understand why society at large would view minorities negatively. Many writers have portrayed ethnic minorities as being from unstable families, having negative value systems, incapable of being assimilated, pathological, promiscuous, racially inferior, sexually aggressive, genetically deficient, culturally deficient, intellectually inferior, externally motivated, treacherous, and having low self-concepts. Examples are easy to find, even today. Recently, a well-known sports analyst indicated that African-American athletes had strong bodies and weak minds, and another sports personality suggested that African-Americans do not have the intelligence to manage large athletic programs.

Images of the Black male as dangerous and treacherous have been common in the media over the past few years. Pictures of the Black male with wide eyes appear in newspapers across America for having either raped, robbed, or murdered. The Black male, therefore, is dangerous, and is to be feared and avoided in every way possible. Given this scenario, how are students to differentiate between Black males they meet on campus and those they meet through the media image?

Many college students have had negative encounters with persons from different cultural or racial groups and have difficulty overcoming those experiences. White students have often had negative encounters with minority students. Some students recall being roughed up or intimidated by groups of minority students in middle or high school. They have often developed strong negative attitudes from these experiences.

Images of Gays and Lesbians are also far from positive in our literature and in the media. Happy and successful Gays and Lesbians are seldom portrayed; the "dyke" image of Lesbians and the "mincing, effeminate" portrayal of Gay men is all too common.

On the other hand, many minority students have had, and continue to have, negative experiences with White/majority individuals that hinder relations. Not only do minority students have historically negative experiences with White/majority individuals, they often encounter day-to-day experiences of racism and prejudice that reinforce their negative attitudes.

Perceived Preferential Treatment

Another barrier to multicultural relations is perceived preferential treatment, wherein each group believes the other has an unfair advantage. Programs such as Affirmative Action, Black Student Union, Minority Fellowship Program, etc., do not seem fair to many White/majority students. One student typified this sort of view when commenting, "It doesn't seem fair that minorities get all the breaks when I have to bust my butt to make ends meet." A few White students object to Black students being able to have a Black Student Union on campus. Recently, a small group of White students on one large southeastern university campus responded by organizing a White Student Union. The White Student Union was to meet the same needs of White students as the Black Student Union does for Black students. Specifically, the organizer of the White Student Union stated that the purpose of the group was to counterbalance the one-sided views of groups like the Black Student Union. Essentially, supporters of the White group included students who felt that minorities were receiving unfair advantages over other university students.

On the other hand, ethnic minority students often think White/majority students receive preferential treatment based on the fact that they are in the majority. They believe that White universities were originated by and for White individuals, and that few changes have been made to welcome and accommodate the needs, unique life-styles, and cultural practices of newcomers (minorities) to the university campus. Minorities also think that the White students' greatest advantage is their perceived power and influence, making it possible to control elections in student government and other campus organizations.

Hispanic, Asian, and Native American students sometimes think that the advantages of minority status are limited to Black students, especially regarding admission procedures and financial aid opportunities. These perceptions of preferential treatment persist and are barriers to multicultural relations.

Homophobia

The general negative attitude that our culture has toward homosexuality is certainly a major inhibiting factor in relationships between the majority culture and Gay and Lesbian people. Most of us grew up with some level of homophobia (fear and negative feelings) about homosexuality, and it is difficult to overcome these feelings and attitudes. The strength of attitude is apparent when you consider how difficult it is for Gay and Lesbian people to "come out" and be honest about their sexual orientation. Often a great deal of pain is associated with this process, and sometimes parents even disown their own children because they are Gay or Lesbian. This is, indeed, a powerful inhibiting force to overcome, on both a rational and a personal level.

FACILITATIVE FORCES

Although many inhibiting factors exist, several factors facilitate the development of CEP's: (1) Self-knowledge, (2) Cultural Knowledge, and (3) Racial/Ethnic Security.

Self-knowledge

> "To thine own self be true and it shall follow as the day the night, thou cans't not be false to any man."
> Shakespeare

Knowledge and awareness about oneself is generally related to one's degree of success and level of functioning. Self-knowledge has been linked to success in educational choice, career choice, athletic performance, and development of interpersonal and multicultural relations. Students who know themselves well in terms of their personalities, needs, and interests are usually better at selecting appropriate and satisfying careers. Athletes with high self-knowledge perform well because they are aware of their strengths and weaknesses. For example, the best track stars are those who know the relationship between the functioning of their bodies and the timing of given events. Sports commentators say that Larry Bird, the premier forward of the Boston Celtics basketball team, makes up for his lack of quickness on the floor by placing himself in certain strategic positions that enable him to score points and get rebounds.

Self-knowledge is also useful in multicultural relations. It gives you the ability to interact effectively across cultural lines and to appreciate cultural differences. Knowledge about your *own* attitudes, feelings, and beliefs concerning cultural differences is the first step toward bridging cultural gaps among groups. Understanding your own hang-ups and idiosyncrasies is crucial for personal growth and for developing empathy for culturally diverse groups. Knowledge about racial identity is also useful in helping people understand their own and others' racial feelings and attitudes.

The understanding and knowledge you have gained by studying the White Racial Consciousness Model, the Minority Identity Development Model and the Gay and Lesbian Identity Development Model (see Chapter 2) will be particularly helpful. By learning about people who are different, you learn more about your own ethnic and/or racial identity. In other words, you get to know yourself better by seeing how you are like or not like other people. Self-knowledge is an end in itself, and is also a means to an end.

Cultural Knowledge

> "Herein lies the tragedy of the age . . . that men know
> so little of men."
> W. E. Burghardt Dubois, *Souls of Black Folk,* 1903.

Cultural knowledge usually includes an understanding of the history, sociology, psychology, economics, customs, traditions, language, and life-style of any group of people. It includes your awareness of the backgrounds, histories, life-styles, and unique characteristics of culturally diverse individuals and groups in your university environment. Cultural knowledge increases appreciation and communication among students in multicultural settings.

Culturally effective persons are knowledgeable about the cultures of groups different from their own. In particular, they are knowledgeable and sensitive to the obstacles and problems that various other groups encounter. Cultural awareness indicates that you are interested in other groups and care about their welfare. This interest and caring can make a difference. For example, the authors have observed that students from foreign countries tend to adjust to campus life more easily, make friends with Americans more quickly, become less isolated, and learn to speak English with greater facility when American students express interest in their cultures. Recently, students from several foreign countries were asked to serve as panel members to discuss certain unique characteristics of their peoples and countries. The more interest the American students showed in their countries, the more the foreign panel members spoke with pride and confidence.

While cultural knowledge is important in multicultural relations, the acquisition of knowledge can be a difficult task. Several exciting and interesting methods can be used to gain cultural knowledge. These include (1) reading ethnic/cultural literature that reflects the values, cultural practices, customs, and traditions of various ethnic groups; (2) touring culturally different communities; (3) attending ethnic churches; (4) interviewing culturally different leaders; and (5) living in the homes of ethnic persons for periods of time (Parker, Valley, & Geary, 1986). Some college students have acquired cultural knowledge by intentionally selecting culturally different roommates or by joining other groups to learn more about their cultures. Some of these students report that, while they learn a good deal, they often experience conflict and doubt. For example, a Cuban student attended a social affair sponsored by a Black student group. He recalled that before attending the affair he had never been so anxious in his life. To his surprise, he was warmly accepted, was not bothered by anyone, and had a great time. Similarly, minority students who join mostly-White organizations often report being received with open arms, and straight students who attend Gay social events have fun and usually have no problem feeling accepted.

Racial/Ethnic Security

Students cannot develop positive multicultural relationships with members of other racial/ethnic groups if they are uncertain or insecure in their own ethnic identity. Ethnic minorities who are secure with their own ethnic identity have resolved conflicts and confusion regarding loyalty to their own ethnic/ cultural groups and their individual autonomy. In addition, such individuals can selectively accept or reject dominant culture values based on previous experience. Students who are secure in their identity accept racial/ethnic/sexual-orientation differences and similarities with appreciation and respect, and seek opportunities for cross-racial interaction. Such students do not perceive differences as deficits and similarities as enhancers (Helms 1984).

Why is racial/ethnic security so important for enhancing multicultural relations on campus? Individuals with strong self-images are generally able to get along with others. Students with strong cultural/racial self-images are more objective and less opinionated on issues concerning race. Such persons can engage in dialogue with members of diverse groups and remain open to issues and concerns without bias or prejudice, and are better able to seek the truth. Such persons can effectively explore issues and questions like, "Should racial quotas be considered in student government elections? Should special services programs exist for minority students? Should a White Student Union or a Gay Student Union be on campus? Racially and ethnically insecure students cannot discuss these potentially sensitive issues without prejudice and anger and, in some cases, even violence.

SUMMARY

As you have seen, many forces inhibit better multicultural relations on campus. Cultural values, racial/ethnic identity attitudes, negative perceptions and experiences, perceived preferential treatment, and homophobia are all powerful and difficult forces to overcome. On the other hand, increased self-awareness, knowledge and understanding about cultures and cultural differences, and security in your own racial/cultural/sexual identity can help you overcome these barriers to better multicultural understanding.

ACTIVITIES

The final section of this chapter is a series of activities designed to help you (1) understand yourself with regard to your relationship with significant others, (2) develop culturally sensitive behavior, (3) model culturally effective behavior, and (4) share cultural knowledge.

ACTIVITY 5-1
Table of Significant Others (TOSO)

Objectives

1. To help you become more aware of significant others and their influences on your personal development.

2. To help you understand yourself better in relation to significant others in your life.

3. To help you become more aware of how you select significant others.

4. To help you examine your feelings about selection of significant others.

5. To help you increase or expand your circle of friends.

Directions for Participants

1. Draw a table with six positions and accompanying lines similar to what is shown in Figure 5.

2. In the space labeled "yourself," write your name. In the space labeled "Primary Significant Other," write the name of the most influential person in your life, *not* including *family* or *relatives;* then continue listing names of significant others by numbers two through five. Be sure to identify only persons who are not members of your family or relatives.

3. On the first line, adjacent to their names, write their *ages.* On the second line, write their *socioeconomic status* (lower, middle or upper-class). On the third line, write their *educational level* (i.e., high school graduate, college graduate, graduate school, advanced graduate study). On the fourth line, write their *sexual orientation* (heterosexual, Gay/Lesbian, or other). On the fifth line, write their *racial/ethnic* identification (i.e., Hispanic-American, Native-American, Asian-American, African-American, or White-American).

Figure 5
TABLE OF SIGNIFICANT OTHERS

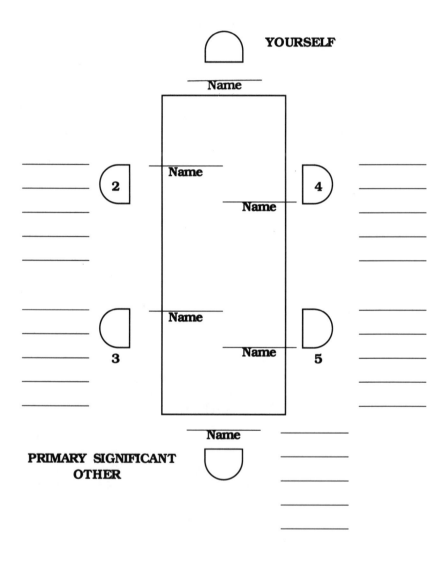

YOURSELF

Name

Name

2

4

Name

Name

3

Name

5

Name

PRIMARY SIGNIFICANT
OTHER

Directions for Group Leaders

Divide participants into small groups of five to seven persons to discuss individual responses to the TOSO (Table of Significant Others). Appoint student leaders for each small group and ask them to lead the discussion based on the following questions:

1. Who are the people at your table of significant others and how did you select them? Under what circumstances did these relationships develop?

2. What is the age range of the people at your table? How similar or different are their ages to your own age?

3. What is the socioeconomic status of people at your table? How similar or different are their statuses to your own?

4. What is the educational level of people at your table? How similar or different are their education levels to your own?

5. What is the sexual orientation of people at your table? How similar or different are their sexual orientations to your own?

6. What is the ethnic/racial identification of people at your table? How similar or different are their ethnic/racial identifications to your own?

7. Overall, to what extent does diversity exist among people you have determined to be significant others in your life?

8. What opportunities or lack of opportunities for diversity existed during your life experiences?

9. What are your feelings and thoughts about people at your table of significant others, and in what ways (if any) would you like to change them?

10. How is your table of significant others similar to, or different from, other students in the group?

11. In what practical ways can you expand individuals at your table of significant others to include people whose cultural backgrounds or whose sexual orientations are different from your own? Please be as specific as possible.

ACTIVITY 5-2
Developing Culturally Sensitive Behavior

Objectives

1. To help you become more aware of the range of multicultural experiences that exist among students on college campuses.

2. To help you identify and understand the difference between cross-cultural sensitivity and cross-cultural insensitivity.

3. To help you identify ways to become more cross-culturally effective.

Directions for Participants

Listed below is a series of campus scenarios where people demonstrate varying degrees of cultural sensitivity toward others. Each scenario has a main character. Read each scenario and rate the extent of each main character's sensitivity (0=least and 5=most). Now join a small group and do the following:

1. Discuss your overall impressions of the scenarios.

2. Compare and contrast your rank with other group members.

3. After discussion, arrive at group consensus on the rankings for each scenario.

4. Discuss ways that the various characters could become more culturally effective.

Campus Scenarios

Scenario One

Janet, the president of a predominantly White sorority, sees herself as open-minded, knowledgeable, and generally sophisticated. Recently, while serving as a panel member on a diversity task force, she was asked why her sorority did not have any Black or ethnic minority members. She responded by saying, "We would really like to have minority members. However, we want to be certain they will be comfortable and would fit in. We also select members whose needs can be clearly met through our sorority."

Scenario Two

Chief Bradford is the new Chief of Police for the University Police Department. The Chief's major goal is the safety, welfare, and security of faculty, students, and other personnel of the University. Her general philosophy of police work is embodied in the quote, "An ounce of prevention is worth a pound of cure." In this regard, the Chief has ordered several of her key officers to carefully patrol the section of campus where Gay students congregate.

Scenario Three

Mr. Oakley, an academic adviser, has a reputation for providing accurate information and for directing students toward appropriate course schedules. While Mr. Oakley is primarily responsible for academic advisement, students often present other issues and concerns to him. These other issues recently included a series of complaints that a new math professor was telling racist jokes in his lectures. Mr. Oakley tells the complaining students that they should be more concerned with learning math skills and should spend less energy dealing with personal attitudes and feelings.

Scenario Four

Reverend Miller, the campus minister, is well known for being outspoken about social issues such as abortion, capital punishment, human rights, and many others. He believes strongly that all individuals and groups have rights to their opinions and that their opinions should be heard and respected. Last month, two students walked into Reverend Miller's office and asked him if he would serve in the official capacity as Adviser for the newly organized White Student Union. Reverend Miller explained to the students that, while he respected their efforts, he could not serve as their adviser because in so doing he would be hindering multicultural relations on campus.

Scenario Five

Dr. Jamison has served as the Chairperson of the Admissions Committee for many years and has a reputation for being honest and fair. Recently, he has been asked to relax his position in order to increase minority student enrollment. Dr. Jamison responded by stating that he understands the circumstances of minority students not meeting admission standards. However, if they were asking him to become inconsistent in executing admissions policy, he would resign as Chairperson of the Admissions Committee.

Scenario Six

Dr. Hwang is a Counselor in the University Counseling Center where she has developed an outreach program for Asian students. One afternoon while Dr. Hwang was in the middle of one of her counseling sessions, she heard a loud knock on her door. She opened the door and the secretary said, "You'd better come quickly because one of the Asian students is in the lobby and she is really upset and I don't know what to do." Dr. Hwang replied, "I am sorry, but you must find someone else to see her because I am in the middle of some very important work with the student I am seeing now."

Scenario Seven

Dean Carson of Academic Affairs is concerned with the quality of teaching and the level of learning in the University. One day some African-American students complained that Dr. Henry, a history instructor, says "Nigra" when pronouncing the word "Negro," and besides, they prefer to be called African-Americans. After hearing the complaint, the Dean told them that he would speak with the faculty concerning cultural awareness.

Directions for Group Leaders

Have all groups present their findings on one large chart so that all the results can be seen together and compared. (Have the results placed on poster board or a large sheet of paper in a format similar to Figure 6.) Conduct a general discussion based on the following:

1. Identify and discuss some of the general themes that emerged during small group discussion.

2. Discuss how each group reached consensus.

3. Identify and discuss scenarios where the main characters were least cross-culturally effective and discuss the characters participants viewed as most cross-culturally effective.

4. Summarize some of the ways main characters in the scenarios could have been more cross-culturally effective.

Place participants in the same small heterogeneous groups and have them share what they learned from the activity and what they are inclined to do next.

Figure 6
GROUP RANKINGS FOR DEVELOPING CULTURALLY EFFECTIVE BEHAVIOR

GROUPS

	I	II	III	IV	V	VI	VII	VIII	IX	X
1.										
2.										
3.										
4.										
5.										
6.										
7.										

SCENARIOS

Rank Each Scenario

1 Least Culturally Sensitive
2
3 Moderately Culturally Sensitive
4
5 Most Culturally Sensitive

ACTIVITY 5-3
Doing the Right Thing

Objectives

1. To help participants model culturally effective behavior.

2. To help participants learn culturally effective behavior through observation.

Directions for Participants

1. Work in small heterogeneous groups (7 to 9 members) and discuss situations or experiences you believe were multiculturally effective on your college campus.

2. Identify a desired culturally effective experience and develop a role-play of a campus scene that illustrates culturally effective behavior. Ask each group member to participate in the development of each scene, and assign various roles to members.

3. After your group has developed the scenario and has assigned roles, rehearse your role-play and wait for directions from the group leader.

4. Each small group acts out the role in front of the large group and asks them what about each scene made it cross-culturally effective. (Be creative but not too obvious.)

Directions for Group Leaders

Have groups act out their roles in front of the entire group. After each small group role-plays, ask the larger group the following:

1. What culturally effective qualities were illustrated?

2. How have they experienced similar situations and how did they respond to them?

3. How might they restructure the role-play to improve cultural effectiveness on campus?

4. What have they learned from the activity?

ACTIVITY 5-4
Intergroup Sharing of Cultural Knowledge

Objectives

1. To help you learn about other cultures and to help others learn about you.

2. To help you gain confidence through intercultural self-disclosure.

Directions for Participants

1. Each of you should work in a small homogeneous group of 7 to 9 members (i.e., Gay/Lesbian, Asian-American, African-American, Hispanic-American, Native-American, White/majority students, etc.).

2. Generate a list of five things *you want others to know about your cultural group.* (Write list on newsprint.)

3. Generate a list of five things *you would like to know about groups different from your own.*

4. Finally, generate a number of ways or methods that others can use to better know your group (e.g., certain novels to read, movies to see, people to contact personally, etc.).

Directions for Group Leaders

1. Ask members of each group to share the list of five things they want others to know about their group and ways to gain additional knowledge.

2. Have them compare and contrast the knowledge generated from each group.

3. Ask them to think about what they learned from each group that was most surprising.

4. Ask each group to take center stage, where members of other cultures may be allowed to raise questions about their culture.

REFERENCES

Atkinson, D. R., Morten, G., & Sue, D. W. (1979). *Counseling American minorities: A cross-cultural perspective.* Dubuque, IA: W. C. Brown.

Brislin, R. S., Cushner, K., Cherrie, C., & Young, M. (1986). *Intercultural interaction: A practical guide.* Beverly Hills, CA: Sage.

Dubois, W.E.B. (1903/Reprint 1929). *Souls of Black folk; Essay and sketches.* Chicago, IL: A.C. McClurg and Co.

Helms, J. (1984). Toward a theoretical explanation of the effects of race on counseling: A Black and White model. *The Counseling Psychologist, 12* (4), 153-163.

Parker, W. M., Valley, M., & Geary, C. (1986). Acquiring cultural knowledge: A multifaceted approach. *Counselor Education and Supervision, 26 (1), 61-71.*

Chapter **6**

MULTICULTURAL COMMUNICATION ON CAMPUS

The world is, indeed, getting smaller and smaller. Advancements in communication and transportation allow people to communicate with each other and travel from one continent to another in incredibly short periods of time. News events that take place in any part of the world are beamed by satellite to the rest of the world instantaneously. Business and industry are rapidly becoming international enterprises.

Because we are becoming so interdependent, we must all (from various cultural backgrounds) communicate more effectively. One training ground for international and intercultural communication is the university or college campus where students, faculty, and staff from many racial/cultural groups come together daily. One university president referred to his campus as an international fish bowl with many opportunities to learn about other cultures. He reported that his university included 1,600 foreign students representing 108 countries, American students from all the 50 states, 2,000 Black students, 1,700 Hispanic students, 1,012 Asian students, 66 American Indian students, and 27,577 White students from a variety of other cultural and economic backgrounds. Among this kind of a large university population, diversity exists in terms of gender, age, race, religion, ethnicity, culture, sexual orientation, geography, economics, and many other factors.

Opportunities for you, as a student, to learn from others cannot occur without effective communication. Effective cross-cultural communication is broadly defined as any interaction involving two or more speakers who are different from one another based on racial or cultural differences. In order to help you examine and develop your own multicultural communication skills, we will follow a model in this chapter similar to the last, examining first the barriers or difficulties related to good multicultural communication and then facilitating factors. Much of this chapter contains information from interviews with students regarding multicultural communication. A model that was originally developed for cross-cultural counseling is also presented and used for skill building.

BARRIERS

A number of barriers to cross-cultural communication are frequently discussed by experts and are also identified by students, faculty, and staff on college campuses. Barna (1988) outlined and discussed several of these barriers or stumbling blocks to cross-cultural communication which include: assumed similarities, nonverbal misinterpretations, preconceptions and stereotypes, tendency to evaluate, and high anxiety.

Assumed Similarities

Barna (1988) contended that, while people within cultures and from different cultures share many commonalities, their expressions and behaviors are strongly influenced by their culture. Making the assumption that everybody is alike shows disregard for cultural uniqueness and sends a message that specific cultural contributions are not valued or appreciated. Barna reported that many college professors err when they assume that foreign students understand their lectures because the students speak English. Unfortunately, many of the English-speaking foreign students only partially understand the lectures. She believed also, that as long as people operate on the assumed-similarity premise, they will not have to face the responsibility of learning about differences.

Nonverbal Misinterpretations

Barna's second barrier to cross-cultural communication is nonverbal misinterpretation. This occurs when individuals from different cultures come together and interpret experiences from their own cultural backgrounds. Each culture has a set of symbols that communicates ideas and meanings among members of the culture, and the lack of understanding of these nonverbal signs, symbols, gestures, and other body movements causes barriers to cross-cultural communication. One example of misinterpretation is the meaning of eye contact from one culture to another. Good eye-to-eye contact is a sign of assertive behavior among Westerners. Yet, among other groups, when one speaker looks down in the presence of another it is a sign of respect. Some Asian students find it bizarre that strangers in America smile and speak to people they do not know. In their cultures, smiles and small talk are usually reserved for close personal friends.

Preconceptions and Stereotypes

Preconceptions and stereotypes, a third barrier, can interfere with good multicultural communication. In Chapter 3, you learned that people often relate to one another based on stereotypes, which are general classifications of groups with disregard for individual differences. People stereotype others as a means of categorizing and predicting behavior, or to explain behavior in unknown groups. Foreign students are often labeled and misunderstood because of stereotyping. For instance, an Arab female student reported that some Americans expect her to be one of several of her husband's wives, since polygamy is practiced in some traditional Arab families.

Stereotypes block communication because they interfere with objectivity. They are not easy to overcome or correct, even with the presentation of counterevidence. They prevail because they are well established and are often used to rationalize prejudice.

Tendency to Evaluate

The fourth barrier, according to Barna, is the tendency to evaluate others rather than attempt to understand them and their world view. Often, each group interprets life from its perspective and believes its view is correct. This can lead to cultural bias and can close off learning and communication possibilities. This evaluation happens frequently among various groups on college campuses.

High Anxiety

The fifth barrier to cross-cultural communication is high anxiety, which Barna believed underlies all the other barriers. While some tension is natural and can be helpful, high anxiety usually debilitates relationships. High anxiety between culturally different individuals causes defensiveness and sometimes leads to depression or even physical illness.

SELECTED REPORTS FROM STUDENTS

The stumbling blocks or barriers to cross-cultural communication discussed by Barna (1988) are similar to those the authors observed from interviewing college students on a large southeastern university campus. The interviews were conducted in small groups by counselors from the university counseling center. The counselors talked with groups of Asian, African, Hispanic American, White/majority, Gay/Lesbian, and foreign students. They were asked to identify barriers to cross-cultural communication on campus and to suggest ways to facilitate communication. Keep in mind that the statements reported are from individual students, and represent their individual feelings and perceptions, not necessarily the feelings and perceptions of all students in that particular group.

Lack of Cultural Knowledge—Cultural Deficiency

The lack of multicultural knowledge was recognized as a barrier to cross-cultural counseling by several students. An Asian student reported that she does not become involved in conversations with White/majority students because she does not understand the subtle nuances of their culture; therefore, she often does not understand the topics being discussed. Her fear of entering into conversations may be misinterpreted as disinterest or antisocial behavior.

Lack of knowledge is often a barrier to cross-cultural communication, even when students have good intentions. For instance, an African-American female student reported that a White girl from one of her classes attempted to use Black jargon with her. She reported that, "A White girl walked up to me and said, 'What's up, my nigger?'" She responded by saying, "What did you say? I'm not your nigger!" The White girl was attempting to demonstrate her lack of prejudice, but her attempt backfired.

One Asian student reported that she was unable to sleep for several days prior to giving an oral presentation in class. Another Asian student talked about how nervous she felt just before she raised her hand to ask a question in class, and how relieved she felt after she responded to a question she had been asked by the professor. Many instructors are unaware of how traumatic it is for some foreign students to talk and participate in class because in many Asian cultures teachers talk, and students listen and take a more passive/ respectful role.

Language

Hispanic students focused on language and their accents as barriers to cross-cultural communication. One student believed that certain foreign accents are more valued than others on American college campuses; i.e., Hispanic accents are viewed as inferior to French or German accents.

A Puerto Rican woman, who was 25 years old when she came to the United States, reported that she initially wanted to get rid of her Hispanic accent because she was ashamed of it. Fortunately, she encountered people who encouraged her to accept herself and her heritage, and now she is proud of her language and her accent. Other students reported that some students made jokes about their accents.

The language barrier among foreign students permeates all other aspects of their lives. For instance, an Asian student had excellent ideas for research papers, but made lower scores than her classmates because she was not able to express her ideas in writing as well as other students. Professors pointed out grammatical errors and did not take into account her limitation in the use of the English language. This student felt that foreign students should not be penalized because of their grammar; rather, they should be supported for their ideas.

Stereotyping

Another barrier to multicultural communication mentioned by students was stereotyping. Almost all groups gave examples of how they had experienced stereotyping on campus. For example, students from South America say that many American students think that all Colombians are drug dealers. A Chinese teaching assistant was told by an angry student that he had no right to give her a "C" in chemistry because Asians only know science and math, and she could make better grades than he in other courses. Yet another student reported that some professors stereotype Asian-American students as having good academic backgrounds, as being hard workers, and as students who study a good deal but who are not creative.

Several Hispanic American and African-American students reported that their White majority friends think they are all on financial aid and were admitted to the university under special admissions criteria. Such categorizations anger them, make them want to withdraw, and, in general, interfere with genuine multicultural communication.

Lack of Tolerance

Here are some of the examples students gave:

An African-American student said that all White students hated Blacks and that no Whites could be trusted.

A Chinese student in Urban Planning was having difficulty with course directives because of a language problem. When she asked the professor for assistance, he told her to read it herself.

A Gay student reported being told that Gays were sinners and that AIDS was punishment from God.

A Black student, president of the Black Student Union, reported that the university had low tolerance toward Blacks. She said, "They aggravate us about our budget, our facilities, our presence, and everything we represent."

A Cuban student with an accent reported that he was told he would need to "lose the accent" if he wanted to be successful in the communications field.

Self-disclosure

Self-disclosure also can be a barrier to cross-cultural communication on campus. Gay students often report problems if they disclose their sexual orientation. One student, who had recently "come out," reported a harassment incident to the campus police, and they responded by saying nothing in the instance was worth reporting. When the student insisted that his problem be heard, laughing occurred in the background.

One student told everyone on his floor that his roommate was Gay. Afterward, whenever the roommate would walk into a room, everyone would get quiet. Many students asked him if he was really Gay. This made him so upset that he eventually moved out of the dormitory. He realized that little or no support for Gay people existed in the dormitories.

Gay and Lesbian students pay a tremendous price when they express their views, true feelings, and beliefs concerning their sexuality. Being open, honest, spontaneous, genuine, and self-disclosing are desired qualities for college students, unless you happen to be Gay or Lesbian.

Denial of Racism

Another barrier to cross-cultural communication mentioned by African-American students is denial. If no awareness of racism exists, then no opportunity is available to solve the problem. African-American students say that many people on campus believe that the problem of racism was solved in the 1960s through the civil rights movement. According to one Black student, many White students think that Black people have arrived and that no contemporary racism exists. One White student believed that Blacks are the leading group in America today. He based his assumption on the fact that Blacks have America rapping, that they are leading in several major sports as well as the entertainment industry, and that they are being elected as mayors in major cities.

Several Black students reported denial of their existence as a barrier to cross-cultural communication. One Black student said, "What bothers me most is some Whites act like Black people don't even exist. They completely ignore the presence of Black people." Another student had similar feelings. He reported, "It has been my experience that Whites will not speak or smile even though you may speak to them first. They simply will not acknowledge your presence."

FACILITATING
MULTICULTURAL COMMUNICATION

Barriers to cross-cultural communication are easier to identify than they are to remove. *Awareness, however, is the first step toward change.* The time is right to improve multicultural relations on campus. A variety of workshops and training experiences, like the ones outlined in this book, can be conducted to improve multicultural relations. The students we interviewed were asked for their suggestions for facilitating multicultural communications on campus, and they offered the following:

1. *Learn about various cultures.* Knowledge of other cultures will increase understanding among people.

2. *Be open and flexible.* In order to improve effective communication, people from all cultures need to be willing to change to accommodate one another. If either side is too rigid and says, "I can't do certain

things because they are contrary to my culture," no communication and understanding can take place.

3. *See others as human.* Students suggested that relations can be improved if people from all cultures are viewed and treated as human beings. When you meet people, ask them about themselves and show an appreciation of their background and culture.

4. *Practice effective communication skills.* Several students stressed the importance of effective communication skills.

5. *Understand your own background and biases.* We are all biased in some ways and we need to admit it and deal with it.

MODELS OF COMMUNICATION

The foundation for multicultural relations on campus is effective communication. One communication model that is particularly helpful for multicultural communication is the triad model developed by Pedersen (1977) to help counselors in training work more effectively with clients from different cultural backgrounds. The model has the major advantage of using members of the client's culture as resource persons for teaching counselors how to work with ethnic clients more effectively. In addition to verbal and nonverbal messages between the counselor and the client, internal or unsaid messages are clarified through Pedersen's pro-counselor and anti-counselor roles. The model uses role-plays consisting of three persons (the counselor-in-training, the client, and a client advocate). According to Pedersen (1977), the triad model works better when both positive and negative feedback are given to the counselors in training. Such feedback is provided by both the anti-counselor and the pro-counselor. Role-plays using the triad model are spontaneous, not scripted.

We have adapted the triad model to help you learn more about general cross-cultural communication. The roles and procedures will be changed to provide learning opportunities for culturally different people to communicate (see Figure 7).

Figure 7
PEDERSON'S TRIAD MODEL
FOR INTERCULTURAL COMMUNICATION

Pedersen's Triad Model	Revision for Intercultural Communication
Client	Sender
Counselor-in-Training	Receiver
Pro-Counselor	Communication Facilitator
Anti-Counselor	Communication Blocker

Study the descriptions of each modified role so that you can play any of them.

Sender

1. Acts out (role-plays) a problem of a person from his or her cultural background. (The problem is not necessarily related to their cultural background.)

2. Shares information about him or herself with the communication facilitator, who is from the same cultural group.

Receiver

1. Uses the most effective communication skills he or she knows, to listen to and demonstrate respect for the sender's thoughts and feelings.

2. Attempts to be as aware as possible of the sender's cultural background.

3. Pays attention to the sender's both verbal and nonverbal messages.

4. Clarifies and summarizes the sender's thoughts and feelings.

Communication Facilitator

1. Helps the receiver and the sender discuss the problems or issues from the sender's cultural perspective.

2. Facilitates the interaction between the sender and receiver.

3. Identifies with the sender (age, sex, socioeconomic background, etc.) and provides cultural information to the receiver.

4. Serves as an on-the-spot resource person who can facilitate communication by providing information the sender may be reluctant to provide.

Communication Blocker

1. Blocks the receiver by pointing out mistakes that he or she might make.

2. Pulls the sender away from the receiver by being judgmental and critical, and planting ideas of distrust in the sender.

3. Represents the negative thoughts of the sender.

4. Forces the receiver to examine his or her own attitudes, feelings, and defensiveness.

5. Directs comments to both the sender and receiver.

6. Hinders communication by getting in between the sender and receiver, both physically and psychologically.

| Example 1 |

Sender (Hispanic Female)

I'm really having trouble with school. I can't seem to please my father. He calls every few days for a report on how I'm doing. I feel under a lot of pressure.

Receiver (White Male)

You do seem anxious. How does all that stress affect you?

Communication Facilitator (Hispanic Female)

(To Receiver)—Remember to take into account the importance of family in most Hispanic cultures. She feels that she has to please her family and stay in close touch with them.

Communication Blocker

(To Sender)—How can this guy understand you? He's never had a Hispanic family. He probably doesn't even care about what you're saying. He probably thinks you should quit school and go back to your family.

(To Receiver)—This woman acts like a ten-year-old. Tell her to stop being so dependent on her family and become an adult. Her father is calling her much too often. Tell her to tell the old man to bug off.

| Example 2 |

Sender (African-American Male)

I'm not sure I made the right decision to attend a predominantly White university. My parents were so hurt and disappointed that I did not attend a historically Black institution, as they did.

Receiver (White Female)

You are doubting your choice to attend this university and you are worried about the effect your decision may have on your relationship with your family.

Communication Facilitator (African-American Male)

(To Receiver)—Many African-Americans of prior generations attended historically Black institutions, where they received strong support and built a strong foundation for positive ethnic identity attitudes. He might be worried that his decision may cause disharmony in his family.

Communication Blocker

(To Sender)—Be careful what you tell this guy. He probably thinks that Black schools are inferior and Blacks should be proud to be attending the more prestigious White universities.

(To Receiver)—Why don't you tell him to tell his parents that he is quite capable of making his own decisions about which university to attend. Besides, don't they realize that predominantly Black institutions are relics of history?

You will have an opportunity to try out this communication model in several of the following activities.

ACTIVITY 6-1
Getting Acquainted

Objectives

1. To help you become better acquainted with your own and other participants' cultural backgrounds.

2. To help you become more comfortable with intercultural communication through reviewing the four roles outlined in the triad model.

3. To help you learn to use the triad model as a vehicle to improving multicultural communications and relations.

Directions for Participants

1. Review the roles of *Sender, Receiver, Communication Facilitator,* and *Communication Blocker.*

2. Study each role carefully and think about how you would play each role in a multicultural interaction role-play.

3. You will be divided into a number of small groups consisting of three members each. Two of the three members will come from similar cultural/ethnic backgrounds or orientations (e.g., two African-Americans), and the third member will represent a person from a different cultural group (e.g., a White American). After all groups are formed, members will select roles to play using the triad model: sender, receiver, and facilitator. Then, the two members of similar cultures (sender and facilitator) will select a problem or issue to discuss with the third member (the receiver). The role of communication blocker is optional and may be used after you have become more comfortable with the first three roles.

4. Select one of the following themes to role-play:

    a. A Hispanic student is upset because others laugh at his or her accent.

    b. An African-American student is reluctant to speak in class because of being the only African-American in the class, and because he or she is shy.

    c. A White student wants to be friends with, but is not accepted by, his or her African-American roommate.

    d. A White student has recently become interested in ethnic minority concerns and wants to know how to get involved with them in a meaningful way.

    e. A Cuban male student is embarrassed because his parents call him long distance at his dorm room several nights a week to see how he is doing.

    f. A Colombian female student is very upset because her brother told their parents back home she was living with an American boy.

    g. A Chinese American student has trouble talking with students in the dorm because he or she feels that their backgrounds are so different.

    h. A Native American student has spent several nights without sleep because of worrying about having to give an oral report in one of his or her classes.

    i. A Taiwanese student living in married housing is frustrated because American students, whom he or she and spouse do not know, borrow personal items from them constantly.

j. An African-American male student has been labeled an Oreo because his closest friends are White and because he is a member of a White fraternity.

k. An African-American female believes she is not wanted at the university. She believes she was admitted only to meet affirmative action quotas.

l. A Gay student is hurt and depressed because when he told several fraternity brothers that he was Gay they threatened to kick him out of the fraternity.

m. A Lesbian student who went to see a counselor because she had been experiencing depression became very upset when her counselor suggested that her condition was due to her failure to establish a significant relationship with the opposite sex, and that possibly she was just using the Lesbian life-style to get back at her parents.

n. A Hispanic male student is worried because he thinks he should be working to help his struggling family rather than being in college, since he is the oldest sibling in the family.

o. An African-American male student worries a great deal because he is attending a predominantly White school against his parents' wishes. His parents wanted him to attend a Black school where he could become well-grounded in his Black identity.

p. A White male student is dating an African-American female student and is depressed because both his and her friends have advised against continuing the relationship.

5. After the problem has been selected, begin the role-play. Remember the following roles. (You will not be using the Communication Blocker role in this first part.)

a. **Sender**—Discuss or role-play a problem with the person designated as receiver.

b. **Receiver**—Listen respectfully to the ideas and feelings of the sender. Show as much understanding as possible during the process.

c. **Facilitator**—Help the receiver by providing understanding and knowledge about the sender's background when such knowledge is needed.

6. Three groups of triads come together for a discussion of your experiences.

Directions for Group Discussions

1. Process the first phase of the triad by raising the following questions:

   a. Sender, how did you feel sharing your ideas and feelings with someone from a different cultural group? In addition, to what extent did you feel the receiver understood what you were saying? Finally, what additional comments would you like to make?

   b. Receiver, how did you feel listening to ideas and feelings of a person from a different culture? What impressions did you draw from the brief interaction? Finally, what additional comments would you like to make?

   c. Facilitator, how did you feel in your role as an assistant to the receiver in the communications process? What additional information can you provide to help the receiver understand the sender better?

2. Now, go back to your triads and change roles (i.e., the sender becomes the facilitator and the facilitator becomes the sender). Remember that the sender and

facilitator must come from similar cultural/ethnic backgrounds, and the receiver maintains the same role. The sender should select a different issue or problem to role-play.

3. After ten minutes, repeat the process; only, in this third round, the facilitator should take on the role of Communication Blocker. After about five or ten minutes, go back into groups of nine (three triads) and discuss your reactions to the blocker's role.

Directions for Group Leaders

When you finish each role-play cycle, provide enough structure and direction to allow groups of nine (three triads) to process their experiences. You may want to make up additional discussion questions and/or provide a trained discussion leader for each processing group.

ACTIVITY 6-2
Intercultural Communication:
Blocks and Pathways

Objectives

1. To help you become aware of intercultural communication blocks.

2. To help you become aware of pathways to intercultural communication.

3. To share thoughts and feelings concerning intercultural communication blockers and to give feedback to others concerning their blocks.

4. To help you take some responsibility for improving intercultural communication.

Directions for Participants

1. List the major groups on your campus who are different from you based on ethnicity and sexual orientation (e.g., African-American, Asian American, Hispanic American, and Gay/Lesbian).

2. Then, write one statement that some members of each group sometimes make that hinders intercultural communication. For example, some students have written that the statement Black students make, "It's a Black thing; you can't understand it," hinders communication.

3. Join a small homogeneous group and compile your statements by group (racial/ethnic, sexual orientation, etc.). These lists should be written on large newsprint to be presented for others to see.

4. Discuss your thoughts, feelings, and experiences about statements you listed, and give feedback to others in your group concerning their statements.

Directions for Group Leaders

1. Have all groups present and discuss their list of blocks to the entire group, using one representative as a spokesperson.

2. After all presentations have been made, ask each homogeneous group to formulate and present a plan to eliminate their blocks to intercultural communication. These plans will be pathways for improving intercultural communication.

3. Have each homogeneous group present their list of pathways to the entire group.

4. Now, place participants in heterogeneous groups and direct them to do the following:

    a. Discuss their feelings about the previous activity.

    b. Ask questions about what they would like to know concerning cultural knowledge of others.

    c. Share something positive about their culture to end the activity.

REFERENCES

Barna, L. M. (1988). In Samovar, L. A., and Porter, R. E., *Stumbling Blocks in Intercultural Communication*, (322-329). Belmont, CA: Wadsworth.

Pedersen, P.B. (1977). The Triad Model of Cross Cultural Counseling. *Personnel and Guidance Journal*, 94-100.

Chapter **7**

MULTICULTURAL ACTION PLANNING

Now that you have learned something about your racial/ cultural identity and related attitudes and feelings; considered the issue of stereotyping; become more aware of what it is like for various campus minorities; identified the characteristics of CEP's (culturally effective persons); and developed some skill in multicultural communication; you will need to consider your own commitment to change. Are you willing to set up some goals to help yourself become a more culturally effective person, and are you willing to help develop programs to promote multiculturalism and respect for diversity on your campus?

Hopefully, the answer to these questions is a resounding, "Yes!" As the final step in your growth toward becoming more culturally effective, the information in this chapter will help you structure goals for continuing your growth and improving multicultural attitudes and behavior on your campus.

When students participate in workshops or classes on topics like multiculturalism, they often become excited and energized because of the many new ideas, feelings, and attitudes that they have encountered. Too often, however, the momentum toward growth and development that is generated in these classes and workshops is lost when participants go back to their regular activities and responsibilities. They sometimes just don't follow up on what they have learned and what they intend to do. We hope that you will avoid this pitfall.

GOAL SETTING

To become a culturally effective person you must set goals. Effective goal setting includes several steps.

1. Set up long-term goals that you really believe in and for which you are really motivated.

2. Set up short-term goals or objectives that are doable and that will lead to your larger goal.

3. Work out a time frame for your goal(s).

4. Put your goals in writing and keep track of your progress.

5. Discuss your goals and your progress periodically with a good friend.

6. Revise your short-term goals and objectives if they prove unworkable.

7. Don't give up easily. Expect to have setbacks and failures.

8. If possible, predict the obstacles to your achieving your goals and objectives, and brainstorm how to overcome them.

PERSONAL VERSUS CAMPUS OR SYSTEM GOALS

Personal goals are almost always easier to set up and accomplish than are institutional goals. For personal goals, you are the primary actor and you have basic control over what you do. System-wide goals are much more difficult to manage. In the case of campus-wide goals toward improving the multicultural environment on campus, many different variables are present with which you have to contend. For example, if one of your goals is to increase positive communication between Gay/Lesbian students and straight students, you can more easily improve your own communication than engineer improved communication for groups of people. This is not to say that a system-wide approach isn't useful. In fact, we have included a section on campus-wide action later on. However, as we said in the introduction to this book, our major focus is on you and how your own personal change can affect the campus. If more and more students become CEP's, then eventually the campus climate will change and become more multicultural and receptive to diversity.

REVIEW OF CONTENT— PERSONAL GROWTH AREAS

In thinking about your goals and what you want to set up as future challenges for yourself, consider each of the areas that we have covered as topics. Certainly, awareness of our own racial and cultural identity development and attitudes is crucial. In a sense we are all engaged in increasing self-awareness throughout our lives. As human beings we are complicated organisms, affected by our past and by both unconscious and conscious memories of what we have been told and what we have experienced. In our media-oriented culture we are also constantly affected by what we see and hear in various forms. Clearly, we must struggle with achieving clarity about our own attitudes and beliefs. If you are a member of a racial or cultural minority group, that status and its effect on your life will probably be more obvious to you than if you are a member of the White majority group. Think about how you want to continue to explore your own identity and attitudes toward other groups and cultures.

We have all heard the term "stereotype," and we all engage in stereotyping and generalizing. As you learned earlier, the use of stereotypes is natural and in many ways helps us cope with the vast amounts of data that we must process. Overcoming stereotypic thinking is difficult. The most effective way to do it seems to be getting to know members of the group for which you have stereotypes. If you are afraid of Gay men and believe that they are all promiscuous and superficial, then getting to know some Gay men will help challenge this stereotype. If you believe that Blacks on campus have been admitted because they are Black and that they don't have academic abilities, then getting to know some Black students will challenge your stereotype. Be careful that you don't just take a token approach and then convince yourself that the people you know are exceptions to the general rule. In addition to this action-orientation to reducing stereotypes, self-analysis and talking about your feelings with others you trust can be very helpful.

You have probably learned a great deal about how other groups of people on your campus feel and react to campus life. You may have learned some things that are disturbing and that you find hard to believe, and you may disagree with the conclusions that some of the students have drawn. Hopefully, at several points throughout your work in this program you have thought about what being from a different racial or cultural group is like. In a way, to think this way is confusing because you also have to guard against stereotyping and overgeneralizing. You must remember that the campus is not experienced the same by all members of a particular group. All White majority students or all Gay/Lesbian students do not have the same feelings, yet you can still imagine what it would be like for you if you were in a particular group. If you still have trouble being empathic in this way, then you may need to work on goals in this area.

As you can tell from the many barriers and difficulties, becoming a culturally effective person is not easy. Many factors seem to mitigate against our learning to be more culturally effective. Some of these are a result of our past learning and of society's inability to deal effectively with racism and prejudice. Negative attitudes and feelings toward affirmative action programs are perfect examples. Often many different feelings are connected to this very sensitive topic, and it is clearly a national political issue. It tends to generate emotional responses and is a complex, and in some ways paradoxical, issue that can clearly impede learning and acceptance of racial and cultural differences. You don't have to tackle this rather large issue as part of your personal quest to become more culturally effective, but you should examine your own attitudes and feelings and learn how your beliefs affect your relationships with minority and culturally diverse groups. Similarly, learned homophobic feelings can impact very negatively your progress toward becoming culturally effective in terms of Gay and Lesbian people. Where do you stand on this barrier to multicultural development?

Communication! We have all heard throughout our lives about how important communication is in all sorts of life areas. It is clearly a major factor in multicultural relations. We have to be able to talk with each other and understand each other if we are to make any progress at all. Learning to communicate with other races and cultures often is not easy. Various groups are often suspicious of others who try to befriend them. They wonder about the others' motives. Some groups, like Gay and Lesbian students often cannot even be open about their minority status, so how are other students going to learn to communicate with them? Strong power imbalances interfere with relationships. Minority groups always feel pressured to conform to the White majority, and the White majority students typically don't need to conform to other norms or standards.

Clearly, different races and cultures have difficulty in communicating. One need only examine the current state of the world and journey ever so briefly into history to discover this truism. What can you, as a single college student, do? A quotation from Eleanor Roosevelt comes to mind, "Rather than curse the darkness, light one candle." You must start somewhere, and a college campus is a good place to start. You already have many different races and cultures present (perhaps not in large numbers, but they are there), and you have an atmosphere where learning and personal growth are encouraged and (hopefully) rewarded. You have already taken a giant step by reading this book and completing the associated class or workshop. Keep the momentum going. If we all work together we can truly overcome the darkness of racism, prejudice, discrimination, and intolerance.

ACTIVITY 7-1
Self-assessment

In this activity you will be given some time to examine your own progress in becoming a Culturally Effective Person. You will assess and consider your progress in the following areas: (1) awareness of your own racial/cultural/ethnic identity, (2) stereotyping, (3) understanding specific campus minorities, and (4) identifying personal blocks to communication with those culturally different from yourself.

Objectives

1. To encourage personal assessment in the development of cultural sensitivity.

2. To assist in personal analysis that will lead to plans for positive change.

Directions for Participants

Take 15 to 20 minutes to write a paragraph discussing your assessment of your progress in each of the above listed areas. Don't worry about the form of your writing. This paragraph is only for your own use. Meet with a small, heterogeneous group and discuss your assessment. Group members should help each other clarify self-assessments. The large group will then get back together and each group will share a comment or two about the process of discussing their own self-assessments.

Directions for Group Leaders

If necessary, review the four assessment areas (listed in introductory paragraph to Activity 7-1) and give some examples of how self-assessment might be conducted in each area.

ACTIVITY 7-2
Personal Action Planning

In this activity you will develop a long-term and a short-term goal for each self-assessment area.

Objectives

1. To encourage the development of concrete plans for self-growth.

2. To provide an opportunity for discussion and exchange of ideas on how to make personal changes that will help individuals become more culturally effective.

Directions for Participants

Take 15 to 20 minutes to consider the self-assessment that you did in the previous activity, and list a long-term and a short-term goal for each area. Review the material in the chapter on goals if you need help identifying long- and short-term goals. Discuss your goals with a small group. Ask the group to give you feedback on how you can accomplish these goals and on what they see as the potential blocks and difficulties that you might have.

Directions for Group Leaders

Review the definitions of long- and short-term goals, if necessary, and give some examples. Encourage the structured feedback and give examples (e.g., if a student plans to improve his or her empathy for specific minority groups by learning more about that culture, how will he or she go about it, and what might interfere?).

ACTIVITY 7-3
Action Planning for Campus Progress

Although the focus of this program has been largely on your own personal development, this activity is an opportunity to take a broader look at your campus environment and develop ideas for campus-wide change and programs that will improve the cultural effectiveness of everyone on campus.

Directions for Participants

Start out in small groups of about four to six people. Take about 30 minutes to brainstorm a list of ideas to improve your campus in terms of cultural sensitivity and level of encouragement for students to learn to become more culturally effective. Brainstorming means letting people come up with ideas without judging them. At first, all the ideas that are presented need to be accepted and put on the list. After the initial listing is made, your small group should go back and pick the ten best ideas that were identified. Then each group should merge with another small group, and the two groups should put their lists together and form a combined list of the ten best ideas that the two groups developed. Then the groups of two should combine with other groups of two (so that you have four original groups), and two combined groups should put their lists together and come up with *their* ten best ideas. After that, the entire group should come back together and hear the lists that remain. The next step, if you have time, is to assign a small working group to each idea to discuss implementation.

Directions for Group Leaders

You will need plenty of magic markers and large sheets of paper for this activity. The implementation phase can be as extensive as you wish. You may want to have some follow-up meetings and even set up a task force of interested participants to continue work.

INDEX

INDEX

lack of tolerance 118-9
language 117-8
nonverbal misinterpretations 115
preconceptions 115
self-disclosure 119
stereotypes 115
stereotyping 118
tendency to evaluate 116
Beckham, B. 66, 85
Bendel, P. 75, 85
Bigotry 69
Bisexual 73
Blocker 123-4
communication 123, 124
Bradford, Chief 104
Brainstorm 142
Brislin, R.S. 90, 111

C

Campus minorities
awareness 9
empathy of 9
Carson 106
Case
illustrations 1
Case example
Cuban 18
Roberto 18
Cass, V.C. 16,23,31,50
CEP (culturally effective persons)
87-111, 137
Cherrie, C. 90, 111
Childhood Message Chart, *Figure* 82
Communciations
lack of multicultural knowledge
116-7
Communication 139
barriers 114-6
blocker 123, 124
cross-cultural 9
facilitating 120-1
facilitator 123, 124, 125, 129
intercultural, *Figure* 122
models of 121-5
multicultural 113-34
on campus 113-34
Conformity
stage one in MID 17, 27

Contact
stage one in WRCM 20-1, 29
Cross-cultural 3
Cross-cultural comunication
definition 7
Cross-racial 3
CSP (culturally sensitive persons)
5
Cultural encapsulation
definition 8
Culturally different group
definition 7
Culturally effective persons (CEP)
87-111
definition 7
Culturally sensitive persons (CSP)
5
Cushner, K. 90, 111

D

D'Augelli, A.R. 73, 85
Dear Abby 78-80
Definitions 6-8
Disintegration
stage two in WRCM 21-2, 29
Dislikes 91-2
Dissonance
stage two in MID 17-8, 27
Dubois, W.E.B. 95, 111

E

Empathy
awareness of 65-85
campus minorities 9
Ethnic minority
definition 6
Ethnocentrism
definition 7, 53
Evaluate
tendency 116
Experiences
negative 92-3

F

Facilitator
communication 123, 124, 125,
129
information for 10-1

Fassinger, R.E. 23, 31, 50
Fields, C. 70, 85
Fiske, E. 71, 85
Forces
    facilitative 94-8
    inhibiting 88-94
Freedman, D. 69, 85

G

Gay and Lesbian Identity
  Development Model (GIDM) 16,
  23-6, 33-41, 95, *Figure* 31
Gay students 3, 4, 73-6
Geary, C. 96, 111
GIDM (Gay and Lesbian Identity
  Development Model) 16, 23-6,
  33-41, 95, *Figure* 31
Goals 9-10
    personal 136-7
    setting 136
    system-wide 136-7
Growth areas
    personal 137-9

H

Helms, J. 87, 91, 97, 111
Helms, J.E. 16, 20, 22, 23, 50
Herek, G. 74, 85
Hispanic student 3, 70-2
Homophobia 75, 94, 139
Hsia, J. 72, 85
Hughes, M.S. 2-3,14
Hwang, Dr. 105

I

Identification
    ethnic 16
    racial 16
Identity
    development 15-50
    racial/ethnic 90-2
Identity acceptance
    stage four in GIDM 25, 31
Identity comparison
    stage two in GIDM 24-5, 31

Identity confusion
    stage one in GIDM 24, 31
Identity pride
    stage five in GIDM 25-6, 31
Identity synthesis
    stage six in GIDM 26, 31
Identity tolerance
    stage three in GIDM 25, 31
Information
    for organizers 10-1
    for faciitators 10-1
Introduction 1-14
Introspection
    stage four in MID 19,28
Ivey, A. 21, 50

J

Jamison, Dr. 105
Janet 104
JAP (Jewish American Princess) 3
Jewish student 3, 68-70
Johnston, D. 68, 69, 85

K

Katz, J.H. 21, 50
Knowledge
    acquisition of 96
    cultural 95-7
    self 94-5

L

Language 117-8
Legitimization 2
Lesbian and Gay students 73-6
Lesbian students 3, 4
Likes 91-2
Lippman, W. 51, 63
Lloyd, A. 5, 14

M

Magner, D. 73, 85
Meeting
    format 10-1

Samovar, L.A. 114, 116, 133
Scenarios 104-6
Scott, J. 77, 85
Security
    racial/ethnic 97
Self-disclosure 119
Self-knowledge 94-5
Self-understanding
    vehicle 16
Sender 122, 123, 124, 129
Sensitivity
    developing 9, 87-111
Similarities
    assumed barriers 114
Smith, E.M.J., 16, 50
Steele, S. 1, 14
Stereotype 9, 51-63, 118, 137-8
    background 51-2
    definition 7-8, 51
    overcoming 54
    process 52-3
Students
    selected reports 116-20
Sue, D.W. 16, 27, 50, 87-8, 91, 111
Symbolic 90

T

Tachibana, J. 67, 85
Table of significant others 99,
    101-2, *Figure* 100

Taylor, C. 2, 14
Tokenism 91
Tolerance
    lack of 118-9
Training
    model 8-9
Treatment
    perceived preferential 93-4

V

Valley, M. 96, 111
Values
    cultural 88-90

W

White Racial Consciousness Model
    (WRCM) 16, 20-3, 26, 33-41, 43,
    95, *Figure* 29-30
Wiener, J. 2, 14
Wittmer, J. 77, 85
Work force 4
WRCM (White Racial Consciousness
    Model) 16, 20-3, 26, 33-41, 43,
    95, *Figure* 29-30

Y

Young, M. 90, 111

ABOUT THE AUTHORS

Woodrow M. Parker, Ph.D., is a Professor of Education in the Counselor Education Department and serves as an affiliate staff member in the Counseling Center at the University of Florida, Gainesville, Florida. He teaches a course, conducts research, writes journal articles and books, and provides a variety of consultation services on Multicultural Counseling. His most recent research involves the development of an instrument to assess cultural knowledge and awareness of African-Americans, Hispanic-Americans, Native Americans, and Asian Americans.

Dr. Parker holds the distinguished honor of having been the most prolific contributor to the *Journal of Multicultural Counseling and Development* from 1982-1987.

Dr. Parker's degrees and positions: BA—Stillman College; MA—University of South Florida; and Ph.D.—University of Florida.

James Archer Jr., Ph.D., ABPP is Director of the Counseling Center at the University of Florida and a Professor in Counselor Education and Psychology. With a colleague he developed one of the first minority peer counseling programs back in the early 1970s. He has worked with clients and student groups since that time in the area of multicultural awareness. He is past president of the International Association of Counseling Services, past chair of the Association of College and University Counseling Center Directors, and holds a Diplomate in Counseling Psychology from the American Board of Professional Psychology. He has written two other books and is currently researching the effects of single session counseling. He lives in Gainsville with his wife and two teenage sons.

Dr. Archer's degrees and positions: BA—University of Rochester; MA—San Francisco State University; and Ph.D.—Michigan State University.

James E. Scott, Ph.D., is Dean of Student Affairs at the University of Florida. A student affairs administrator for nearly 20 years, he is well respected by professional colleagues. He has been named three times to the Board of Directors of the National Association of Student Personnel Administrators and is currently serving as the National Conference Chairperson for the 1992 NASPA Conference in Cincinnati, Ohio. The father of three college students, ages 18, 19, and 21, he lives in Gainsville, Florida with his wife.

Dr. Scott's degrees and positions: BS, History—Eastern Michigan University; MA, Counseling—Eastern Michigan University; Ph.D., Higher Education Administration—University of Michigan; Post Doctoral Studies—Harvard University.